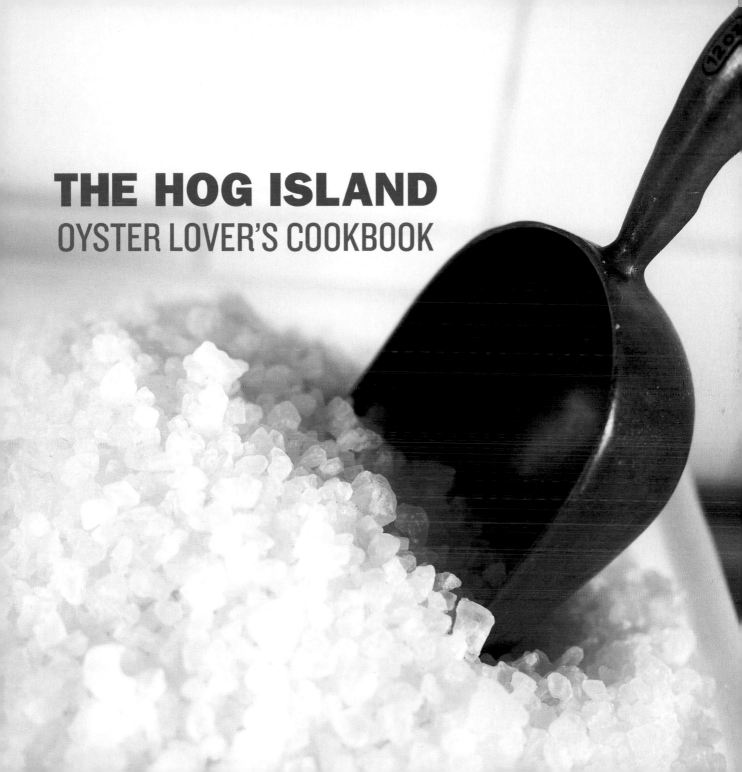

THE HOG ISLAND
OYSTER LOVER'S COOKBOOK

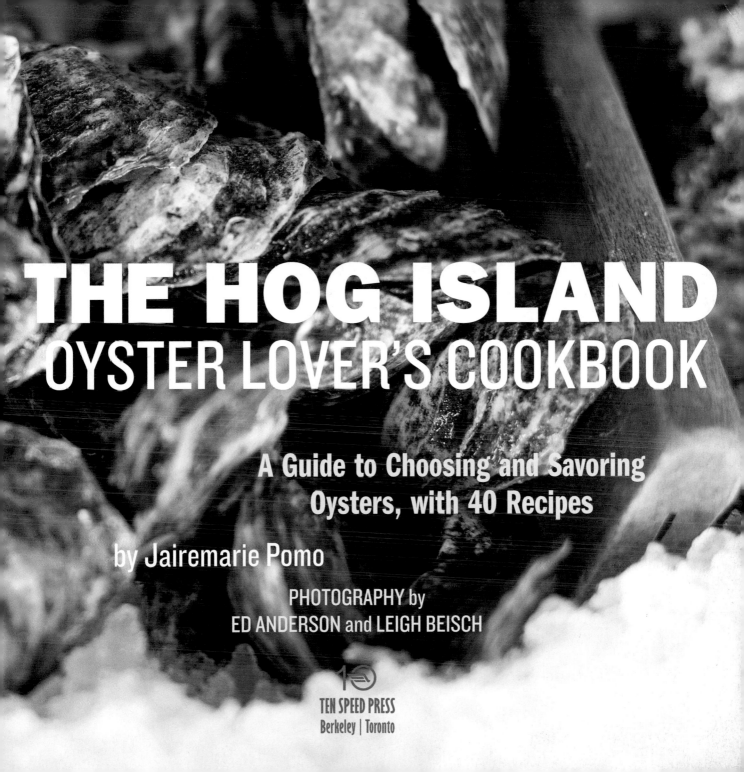

THE HOG ISLAND
OYSTER LOVER'S COOKBOOK

A Guide to Choosing and Savoring
Oysters, with 40 Recipes

by Jairemarie Pomo

PHOTOGRAPHY by
ED ANDERSON and LEIGH BEISCH

TEN SPEED PRESS
Berkeley | Toronto

Ten Speed Press
PO Box 7123
Berkeley, California 94707
www.tenspeed.com

Cover and text design by Toni Tajima
Food styling by Dan Becker
Prop styling by Emma Star Jensen

Distributed in Australia by Simon and Schuster Australia,
in Canada by Ten Speed Press Canada, in New Zealand by
Southern Publishers Group, in South Africa by Real Books,
and in the United Kingdom and Europe by Publishers
Group UK.

Library of Congress Cataloging-in-Publication Data
Pomo, Jairemarie.
   The Hog Island oyster lover's cookbook: a guide to choos-
ing and savoring oysters, with 40 recipes/by Jairemarie
Pomo; photography by Ed Anderson and Leigh Beisch
      p. cm.
   Includes index.
   ISBN-13: 978-1-58008-735-3 (hardcover)
   ISBN-10: 1-58008-735-3 (hardcover)
   1. Cookery (Oysters) 2. Cookery—Hog Island. I. Title.
   TX754.O98P66 2007
   641'.94—dc22

            2006037613

Printed in China
First printing, 2007
1 2 3 4 5 6 7 8 9 10 — 11 10 09 08 07

For my dad, Charles Edward Pomo,
who loved his children and grandchildren,
the ocean, hummingbirds, and oysters.

CONTENTS

introduction   The Hog Island Story | 1

chapter 1   A Mouthful of Oyster History | 11

chapter 2   Introducing Oyster Varieties | 29

chapter 3   Buying, Handling, and Enjoying Oysters | 49

chapter 4   Raw Oysters | 81

chapter 5   Hot Oysters | 109

resources | 156

acknowledgments | 162

index | 164

THE HOG ISLAND STORY

I am standing behind the traveling Hog Island oyster bar set up under an enormous tent at a tony food and wine event in the Napa Valley. The crowd is well-heeled, elegant, and mannered—that is, until they spy the oyster bar. They start lining up ten deep. I hear the familiar buzz: "Hog Island is here—I love Hog Island oysters."

Women approach with flirtatious and seductive body language that suggests they're going after a Calvin Klein underwear model. Men stand at the corners and surreptitiously snatch oysters from the ice. One woman, a glass of Champagne in one hand and a freshly shucked Kumamoto oyster in the other, breathlessly asks Michael Watchorn, cofounder and co-owner of Hog Island Oyster Company, "Is there really a Hog Island?" Without missing a beat, Mike answers, "Hog Island isn't a place, it's a state of mind." That irreverent answer sums up the Hog Island Oyster Company story, the guys who started it, and the incredible success they now enjoy. That "state of mind" is what nurtured the first tiny harvest of oysters in 1984, and it's what drives the company today: a passion for cultivating the best oysters in the country, a real enjoyment in satisfying oyster-lovers, and an ardent commitment to the stewardship of the land and water.

It started in 1979, with two guys from opposite coasts: Mike Watchorn, a marine biology student at the University of California Santa Cruz, and John Finger, a recent graduate of the marine science program at Southhampton College on Long Island. Their lives were about to converge at an oyster-growing operation in Moss Landing, California, a tiny seaside community between Santa Cruz and Monterey.

After graduation, John headed for California and landed a job at International Shellfish Enterprises (ISE), an oyster-growing operation owned by a huge, diversified agricultural business. Situated at Moss Landing, ISE had big plans to grow oysters in Elkhorn Slough, an estuary across the shoreline highway.

It's easy to spot Moss Landing from miles away. Pacific Gas and Electric Company built a power plant there the 1950s, and the 225-foot exhaust towers mar the landscape of the otherwise pristine coastline. Within the shadow of this power plant, John began his career as an oysterman, working as a field supervisor. Disillusioned with a nine-to-five corporate culture that he lobbied to change, he left ISE briefly before being called back to fill the post of operations manager. Later, he managed the company's grow-out leases on Tomales Bay, the future home of Hog Island Oyster Company.

As a student at U.C. Santa Cruz, Mike was spending a lot of time at the Moss Landing Marine Laboratory, and while studying there he learned about a job at ISE, just down the road from the lab. He was hired and did a variety of tasks, from piloting the boats to working on the shaker (a machine that sorted the oysters by size). After a few short months, Mike was recruited to design a system to help the baby oysters survive being transplanted into open water. Together with John, Mike redesigned the existing hatchery system so there was a greater survival rate for the babies. When oysters from the hatchery reached 2 millimeters—about the size of a peppercorn—they were transferred to Mike's "pre-nursery," where they quadrupled in size. The pre-nursery allowed the oysters to grow under controlled conditions before they were moved to trays suspended in Elkhorn Slough.

The two men had more in common than oysters. They were both irreverent and quirky, and had reputations for operating just outside the rules. Together with another marine biologist, they rented a large, colonial-style house in nearby Aptos, where they became famous for their seafood-themed parties. Moss Landing fishermen provided them with massive quantities of free squid, which they served with plenty of beer and loud music. Terry Sawyer, a future partner in Hog Island, attended some of those parties, which were, he says, "memorable."

At ISE, Mike and John were cutting their teeth on oyster aquaculture, sometimes learning how *not* to grow oysters. For example, some of the oysters big enough to transfer to Elkhorn Slough were situated near the warm effluent of the power plant and grew big and fast, which turned out to be a disaster. In warmer water, oysters grow too quickly and don't have time to lay down the thick shell that gives them a longer life out of water. Without the seasonal drop in water temperature necessary for a natural reproductive cycle, their breadth of taste characteristics cannot fully develop. And at the ISE site, the oysters not only grew fast, they also took in some nasty chemicals from the power plant. Thankfully, none of them made it to market.

John and Mike were fortunate to see firsthand how big mistakes were made on a huge scale. These experiences proved to be valuable lessons in the virtue of patience. A few years later, when they established Hog Island, the men found that it takes an entire rotation of seasons and a complete growth cycle before a new site or new growing method can be considered a success. Their persistence and attention to detail is one of the hallmarks of Hog Island today.

One of the better decisions that ISE made was to move their juvenile oysters to Tomales Bay, in western Marin County, for the final stage of the oysters' life before harvesting, called the "grow-out." ISE had leased four hundred acres of bay water, and John oversaw the transfer of the oysters into Tomales Bay. Mike, still working at the ISE Moss Landing site, came to see the Tomales Bay operation. The two soon realized that Tomales Bay, with its pristine waters and history of successful oyster farming, might be the ideal place to start their own oyster farm.

To make sure that they were on the right track, John and Mike took time off to scout other locations around the country. They traveled up the Pacific Coast looking at other oyster farms, fly-fishing along the way. They even went east in the middle of winter to look at historical commercial oyster-growing areas near Chatham, Massachusetts. Mike took one look at oysters poking up through the snow at low tide and proclaimed that Chatham was no place for a California boy.

In the early 1980s, ISE went out of business. Mike went to work for Tomales Bay Oyster Company as their farm manager, and John went to work for Marinelli Shellfish, a San Francisco company that distributed seafood and shellfish to Bay Area restaurants. They saw the growth in demand in the market for high-quality farm-raised West Coast oysters for the half-shell trade, and it fueled their desire to start their own farm. The two men were young and just reckless enough to take a calculated risk, so they scouted Tomales Bay for a location they felt would give them the best conditions to cultivate great oysters: a good tidal flow and nutrient-rich seawater close to a freshwater source that would sweeten their crop.

Their first five-acre lease was right at the mouth of Walker Creek. They had to apply to five agencies before they were granted the lease: the California State Department of Fish and Game, the California Department of Health Services, the Army Corps of Engineers, the California Coastal Commission, and the Marin County Department of Public Health. It was eighteen months before the process was complete. In the interim, they recruited friends, including future partner Terry Sawyer, to scavenge for materials to build their first suspended rack-and-tray aquaculture system. Finally, in November 1982, they were granted the lease.

With $500 borrowed from their parents, the two young oyster farmers purchased fifty thousand oyster spat from a hatchery in Humboldt County and placed them in mesh trays on racks made from recycled materials. With a not-too-seaworthy borrowed sixteen-foot fiberglass skiff they called The Flexible Flyer, they were in business—sort of. Three weeks after they planted their first batch, they pulled up the trays and discovered that the mesh wasn't fine enough and rock crabs had destroyed half of their oysters.

The rack-and-tray system they had developed also turned out to be a problem. The iron-rebar platform supported two wooden frames with nylon mesh trays. Placed about two feet off the bottom of the bay in shallow water, the trays were exposed at low tide, which helped to slow the growth of the oysters—a good thing. But sea lions discovered that the trays were a wonderful place to sun, and thousands of spat were crushed under tons of blubber.

There were other challenges as well. There was no mooring or pier for The Flexible Flyer and they lived with the constant worry that they would lose their borrowed boat to a high tide or a storm. Without the luxury of a shore-side facility, they had to trudge through the mud flats lugging bags of oysters from the boat and flinging them over a seawall so they could sort their crop on a rocky beach. Working only when the tides were low meant being on the bay day or night, rain or shine. They didn't own radios for their boats, and without today's sophisticated GPS technology, they sometimes got lost in the soupy fog, occasionally in the middle of the night. The fierce winter storms that pummel the northern California coast scared the bejeezus out of them on more than one occasion. Mike recalls being on the bay with near-gale force winds that drove the rain horizontally across the oyster beds. In hip boots and wet gear, they slogged through their farm, working their lease and coaxing their oysters to market size.

In spite of the tremendous amount of labor it took to get the farm started, they couldn't quit their day jobs. Mike did double time, working at Tomales Bay Oyster Company as farm manager during the day and running his own traveling-oyster-bar catering business evenings and weekends. John continued to work for Marinelli Shellfish, traveling around the Bay Area and pitching the merits of fresh, high-quality clams and mussels. In doing so, he discovered that most restaurants had been serving eastern cherrystone clams for years, but they were unfamiliar with the sweeter, more tender Manila clam. John saw that there was a market for Manila clams, so he and Mike started growing them on the Hog Island lease. Today, they grow forty thousand pounds of Manila clams—a small number compared to the three million oysters they harvest annually.

While the oysters were growing on the first five acres, Mike and John leased five more acres and, with the wisdom gained from their mistakes, put more Pacific spat into the water. Finally, the oysters from their first five-acre lease were ready to harvest: twenty-five precious bushels of beauti-

Why, then the world's mine oyster, which I with sword will open.

WILLIAM SHAKESPEARE

ful Hog Island Sweetwaters were delivered to Chez Panisse, Zuni Café, and the Pacific Heights Bar and Grill through their new distributor, Marinelli Shellfish.

While Mike and John were learning how to grow oysters, their future partner, Terry Sawyer, was learning how to care for oysters once they were harvested—although he didn't know it then. Terry grew up in a Florida beach community and attended the Rosenstiel School of Marine Science in Miami and U.C. Santa Cruz with a major in marine biology. A few years behind Mike and John, Terry was lured to the new Monterey Bay Aquarium project. There, he worked side by side with renowned aquarists who were using revolutionary technology to create a world-class marine research center and public aquarium. He started as a volunteer, but when offered a full-time position as an aquarist he jumped at the opportunity. In his new role, Terry learned methods critical for providing a healthy environment for marine organisms, a skill set he brought to Hog Island.

Hog Island was doing a booming business in 1988, and most of it was during the stormy winter months, when oyster harvesting could be brought to a screeching halt by regulatory agencies who monitored the quality of bay water affected by run-off. Faced with irregular harvests and a sputtering income, they knew they needed a way to harvest oysters before a heavy rainfall (and subsequent closure) and keep them in an environment that was identical to or better than the bay in order to meet the steady demand in the marketplace. What they needed was a tank or wet-storage system to hold oysters.

John and Mike approached Terry with their idea and proposal. Terry had been working for the Monterey Bay Aquarium for six years. He had a good, steady income and benefits. John and Mike invited Terry to come up to Marshall with the intention of talking him into leaving his secure, cushy job. Terry's initial impression of the Hog Island operation wasn't very inspiring. John and Mike had leased shoreline property that included the old Marshall Store building's pigpen and a colony of squatter-artists. Terry was speechless. But then he saw the oyster beds and the astounding beauty of Tomales Bay, surrounded by acres of national park and near the charming small town of Point Reyes Station, and he was hooked.

The Hog Island offices are still perched on the edge of Tomales Bay and hum with the activity of a busy farm and retail operation. Management and crew, clad in wet gear and hip boots, are in and out of the office all day, checking tides and orders and the maps that detail every square foot of the company's leases. Hog Island oysters long ago became a staple of the high-end California food scene, and their renown is now international. But like good farmers anywhere, the Hog Island guys have never stopped learning about their crop, and have kept working to perfect their methods for producing premium oysters (see page 62 for the story of the current state of the art at Hog Island).

HOW HOG ISLAND OYSTER COMPANY GOT ITS NAME

Hog Island Oyster Company is located on Tomales Bay, a slender finger of water about an hour's drive from San Francisco in western Marin County. From the top of the hill above the town of Olema, near the Point Reyes National Seashore headquarters, you can get a clear view of the bay, a deep blue slash of water that demarcates the North American Plate from the Pacific Plate. As bucolic as the scene appears, below the water dozes the mighty San Andreas Fault, giving the bay its nickname: Earthquake Bay. On the east side of the bay are gently rolling hills, carpeted with seasonal grasses that support hundreds of acres of ranch land; on the west side is misty Inverness Ridge, forested with fir, redwoods, alders, and California bay laurel. Calm as a whisper in the early morning, the bay can turn turbulent by late afternoon as winds rip down the corridor between ridge and hills.

Out near the confluence of bay and ocean is a freckle of land called Hog Island. Local legends claim that the island, which is a little more than two acres in size, was named after a barge broke loose and deposited a posse of pigs there. At low tide, you can walk from Hog Island to a smaller rock outcropping that locals call Piglet.

When John Finger and Michael Watchorn put their first oyster seed in the waters of Tomales Bay, they chose a site between the freshwater Walker Creek and Hog Island. One sunny afternoon, John brought his wife, Debra, up to Tomales Bay to see their new venture. John, Debra, and Mike boarded the farm's rickety boat, The Flexible Flyer, and set out on a tour of the oyster beds.

At the end of the day, they motored over to Hog Island and climbed up to the rocky, flat top to get a bird's-eye view of the oyster beds. From their perch, the three looked down and gasped in horror as they watched their boat drift away from the island with the incoming tide. John sprinted down to the beach, leaving a trail of wet gear and hip boots, plunged into the 50°F water, and frantically swam after the boat. He couldn't overtake it, so the three castaways started yelling toward the east shore, hoping that someone, anyone, would come to their rescue. Thankfully, just before sundown a passing fisherman picked them up.

The next day, reflecting on their odyssey, Mike and John christened their new company Hog Island Shellfish, changing it to Hog Island Oyster Company in the mid-1990s. They were told by more than one well-meaning person, "You can't associate your oyster company with hogs—hogs are dirty and smelly." Well, after a particularly long week of oyster farming, they thought this was a pretty good description of themselves. The name stuck, and today, there are a number of Hog spinoffs: Hogwash, the delicious mignonette topping for raw oysters (see page 84); the Hog Shack, the hub of their on-site retail operation; French Hogs, the European flat oysters they cultivate; and Hog Bags, for toting oysters home from the farm. Today, no one thinks twice about the other kind of hog, and trademarked Hog Island oysters are shipped and proudly served around the country and the world.

CHAPTER 1

A MOUTHFUL OF OYSTER HISTORY

Oysters have been part of human culture in North America for ten thousand years. They were a staple of the Native American diet on the East, West, and Gulf Coasts. Oysters were so plentiful in the estuarine environments and so easy to harvest that entire encampments were built around this food source. Archeologists have identified hundreds of shell middens, or mounds of discarded shells, from New Brunswick, Canada, to Florida; around the Gulf Coast in Texas, Alabama, and Louisiana; and all along the Pacific Northwest coast. Some sites contain millions of shells.

In what is now the state of Maine, along the Damariscotta River, Native Americans feasted on the abundant Eastern oyster, *Crassostrea virginica*, leaving enormous mounds of shells along the banks of this exquisite tidal estuary. These mounds are estimated to be twenty-one hundred years old; even older sites have been found hundreds of miles away along the coast of the Gulf of Mexico. The two oldest shell middens yet discovered in Texas are located near Galveston Bay and document thirty-five hundred years of Native American habitation there. Sites have been excavated from Corpus Christi, Texas, to the Louisiana bayous, providing archeologists with a rich source of information not only about the diet of early Native Americans, but about changes in ancient coastlines, climate, and ecosystems.

On the Pacific Coast, Native Americans enjoyed a hearty diet of oysters as well. The native oyster here is *Ostrea conchaphila*, which is smaller than the Eastern oyster. Along the shores of San Francisco Bay, an astounding number of shell mounds—around 425—have been identified. From the Hog Island Oyster Bar, situated on the western shore of San Francisco Bay, you can look across the water to the site of one of the biggest shell middens in the Bay Area and

An oyster, that marvel of delicacy, that concentration of sapid excellence, that mouthful before all other mouthfuls, who first had faith to believe it, and courage to execute? The exterior is not persuasive.

HENRY WARD BEECHER

possibly all of California. Before it was leveled in 1924 to make way for a paint factory, the mound was 40 feet high and over 350 feet in diameter. When archeologists began excavating in 1999, they found that the lower strata of the mound—about twenty-eight hundred years old—consisted primarily of mussel and oyster shells. Today, a massive IKEA store sits on top of the site. Other sites in central California and on the Channel Islands, just off the coast, are approximately ten thousand years old.

THE ATLANTIC COAST

Oysters had been popular along the coasts of Europe and Britain for centuries, so when Europeans began colonizing the East Coast of North America in the 1600s, they found that they shared a common food heritage with the native peoples there. Scholars have documented that oysters may have helped to save some of the early colonists from starvation in their first hard winters. In February 1623, colonists in Wessagusset, a tiny fishing village and trading post (now Weymouth, Massachusetts), subsisted on clams, nuts, oysters, fish, and stolen corn—actually not a bad diet by today's standards.

Initially, settlers collected oysters themselves or bartered with native peoples. Their foraging and limited harvesting had very little impact on the oyster population. But as more settlers arrived and towns were established, the market for oysters exploded. By 1719, just ninety-six years after the first settlers shucked oysters to keep from starving, the General Assembly of the Province of New Jersey passed a law to protect oysters from being overharvested in Delaware Bay. The law states that no oysters could be harvested between May 10 and September 1, the months when oysters spawn. It also states, in part:

> Oyster beds are being wasted and destroyed by strangers and others at unseasonable times of the year, preservation of which will tend to great benefit of poor people and others inhabiting this province.

This law is the first documented measure of oyster-habitat conservation. It could also very well be the source of the prevailing misinformation about avoiding eating all oysters in months without an "R." While it's true that oysters from the warmer waters of the East Coast and Gulf states should not be eaten during the summer months, oysters from northern California and the Pacific

Northwest can generally be eaten year-round (see page 55).

In spite of similar laws and measures, the oyster populations along East Coast bays and estuaries eventually went into decline. As the coastal towns and cities of the east grew, indigenous oyster beds were threatened with a bevy of troubles.

Emblematic of the tumult of the commercial oyster farming industry is the case of fabled Chesapeake Bay, the largest estuary in the United States: sixty-four thousand square miles of tidal watershed, fed by numerous freshwater streams and rivers. In 1701, a traveler commented that the oyster reefs there were so large and prevalent that they posed a hazard to ships navigating the bay. Commercial oystering in Chesapeake Bay began in earnest in the early 1800s. At its peak in the 1890s, Maryland's oyster fishery yielded four to six million bushels per year, and Virginia recorded massive harvests of nearly ten million bushels annually, making the Chesapeake oyster one of the most popular oysters on the eastern seaboard.

At first, Chesapeake oystermen used enormous hand-held tongs to harvest their prized oysters from the abundant reefs before delivering them to shippers and shucking houses. During the 1880s, as the demand for oysters increased, dredges were introduced that scraped the bay bottom, further disrupting the fragile ecosystem that had sustained the Eastern oyster for thousands of years. Dredging was finally halted in the 1940s, but overharvesting, increasing pollution, and introduced species and diseases caused a massive decline in oyster populations. By the late 1980s, the entire oyster industry (as well as other fisheries) of the Chesapeake had nearly collapsed.

In 1994, the states of Maryland and Virginia, environmental groups, and the local oyster industry collaborated on the Oyster Management Plan, a strategic initiative to restore native oyster populations, and the Chesapeake became one of the first major estuaries in the nation to be targeted for restoration. Other organizations are working collaboratively to restore the entire native habitat of the Chesapeake.

North of the Chesapeake Bay, the waters surrounding Long Island were once one of the most prodigious oyster fisheries in the country. Long Island Sound oyster beds supplied millions of oysters to dining establishments along the East Coast and to the mushrooming population of Manhattan. Along the southern shore of Long Island is Great South Bay, home to the famous Blue Point oyster. This oyster became so well known that oysters from other areas are often labeled "Blue Points," regardless of their geographic source.

Like those of the Chesapeake, however, Long Island oyster fisheries suffered tremendously from pollution. The original people who lived around the shores of Long Island Sound did little to disturb the marine habitats. When Anglo-Europeans began arriving in the 1600s, they found a bounty of shellfish and vibrant, unpolluted waters. In the four hundred years since, the area has become the most densely populated region in the United States, with over eight million people who live or vacation on the Sound. The resulting runoff of industrial pollutants, fertilizers, pesticides, and oil from cars substantially affected water purity and caused a die-off of the once-prodigious oyster population.

Adding to local oystermens' environmental woes is the Sound's unique vulnerability to hurricanes. In 1938, a massive hurricane caused a surge of ocean water to flood into the Sound, which raised the salinity levels and created a suitable environment for the dreaded oyster drill, a marine snail that decimated the remaining native oyster beds. In the 1940s, attempts were made to replant oysters, but by 1960 the same parasites that had attacked the Chesapeake oysters had completely wiped out commercial oystering in Long Island. Today, oysters are

making a comeback thanks to cleaner waters and the development of disease-resistant strains. Modern aquaculture and hatchery operations are helping to keep a $100 million oyster industry alive in the waters off Long Island.

North of Long Island is Cape Cod, the crooked-finger peninsula that defines the eastern edge of Massachusetts as it juts out into the Atlantic. With numerous harbors, inlets, and estuaries for habitat, the waters around Cape Cod are renowned for their oysters. The oldest commercial oyster company in the country was founded in 1837 in Cotuit Bay along Nantucket Sound. Harvested using rakes and buckets, oysters were shipped in barrels to Boston and New York. Perhaps not coincidentally, the oldest continually operating restaurant in this country is Boston's Union Oyster House (established in 1826 as Atwood and Bacon's). During World War II, the military established a landing-craft training camp along this section of Cape Cod and succeeded in smothering the fragile oyster beds with silt churned up from the bottom of the bay. But the Cotuit Bay Oyster Company has survived, with a thirty-three-acre lease and a booming demand for Cotuit oysters.

In the semiprotected waters of Cape Cod Bay (inside the crooked finger of the Cape),

THE INDOMITABLE GULF COAST OYSTER

Oysterers along the Gulf Coast from Florida to Texas harvest *Crassostrea virginica*—the Eastern oyster found all along North America's East Coast. The Gulf fishery exploded in the nineteenth century with the collapse of fisheries along the Atlantic Coast, and by 2000, the Gulf states were producing 83 percent of the Eastern oysters in the country. Already faced with such chronic challenges as the oyster drill, degrading ecosystems, and the warm-water threat of *Vibrio* bacteria (see page 55), the oyster industry in the Gulf suffered a dramatic one-two punch from hurricanes Katrina and Rita in 2005.

On September 24, 2005, just hours before Hurricane Rita made landfall in southwestern Louisiana, I was on the phone with Pat Fahey, owner of AmeriPure, an oyster-processing company in Franklin, Louisiana. It had been less than a month since Hurricane Katrina had ripped through southeastern Louisiana, and I called Pat to find out just how much damage Katrina had wrought on the Gulf's oyster beds. As we talked, in the background I could hear the cacophony of workers battening down for the approaching storm. Pat reported that it was too early to tell just how much damage had been done by Katrina—no one had been able to get to the massive reefs and multiple intertidal estuaries.

Nearly a year later, Pat and I talked again. He reported that the impact on the oystering infrastructure was much worse than what the oysters themselves suffered. Most shucking houses along the Gulf Coast were destroyed; small oystering outfits lost homes and boats; piers and warehouses were either completely destroyed or made unusable by the two big hurricanes. The great Gulf oyster reefs in Louisiana were closed for months, but reopened for limited harvesting in December, 2005.

In spite of Rita's landfall in Texas, most oyster harvesting there was suspended for only a few weeks. The worst damage to the oyster beds was in Mississippi, where nearly all the oyster beds were destroyed by silting or the uplifting of entire reefs by storm surge. Although Mississippi is not a big commercial oyster-producing area, the impact of the two hurricanes will be felt for years to come. Following the hurricanes, marine biologists report that the spat set (the oyster seeds successfully attached to substrate) is very healthy along much of the Gulf Coast. Within a few years, the super-filtering oyster will reclaim its territory, and barring another parade of deadly hurricanes, the species and its habitat will come back.

is Wellfleet. The Plymouth colonists discovered a rich fishing ground in what is now Wellfleet Harbor and named the area Billingsgate after the famous London fish market. In a petition to incorporate the village of Billingsgate, town leaders, hoping to boost shellfish sales, chose the name Wellfleet after the famous Wellfleet or "Wallfleet" oysters of England's Blackwater Bay.

Wellfleet also sounds like "whale fleet," and indeed, whaling was a huge industry in the early 1700s. Around 1770, oysters began to die off in Wellfleet Harbor. Fishermen brought in seed oysters from as far away as the Chesapeake. They took hold, and Wellfleet became the biggest oyster producer in the area. Today, the oyster industry is still thriving, and you don't have to search far to find Wellfleet oysters on the menu—they are shipped around the country and enjoy as much cachet as Blue Points.

Finally, in the northeasternmost corner of the country is Maine, where happily the coastal waters have suffered less damage than those in the more populous areas to the south, although by-products from the timber industry have fouled many river estuaries. In 2002, the Maine legislature passed a bill to protect the uppermost region of the Damariscotta River, creating a marine preserve. A handful of oyster farms there are practicing responsible aquaculture methods, cultivating and harvesting native Eastern oysters and the European flat oyster in small numbers. Oysters are making a comeback here.

THE PACIFIC COAST

While the Eastern oyster was being gobbled up by throngs of Europeans arriving on the East Coast, a different species, the diminutive native Western oyster, *Ostrea conchaphila* (*conchaphila* means "shell lover" in Latin), was flourishing undisturbed on the West Coast. Millions of these little oysters grew in San Francisco Bay and in protected tidal estuaries and inlets all along the Pacific Coast and northward into the temperate regions of southern Alaska. In the deeper waters of California's Tomales Bay and Humboldt Bay, where water is constantly replenished with food by the tidal surge and is well protected from the open ocean, the native Western oyster thrived. The same was true in similar environments farther north—Yaquina Bay in Oregon, Washington's Puget Sound, and among the deeper tidal inlets of British Columbia—but only until the oyster beds were discovered by settlers coming west.

The native Western, or Olympia, oyster had long been one of the primary foods of Native Americans along the coast. The well-

documented shell middens of San Francisco Bay are not the only indicators of the importance of oysters in West Coast Native American culture. The Coast Salish tribe inhabited the area of present-day British Columbia, and oysters were an integral part of their diet and culture. Women were the oyster gatherers, and an individual woman's skill at collecting the mollusks could elevate her status within her tribe. Near Ketchikan, Alaska, in Saxman Village, the Tlingit people created totems to the oyster, and a common saying among the Tlingit, "When the tide goes out, the table is set," refers to the importance of intertidal foods like oysters in their diets. The town of Marshall, California, on Tomales Bay, home to Hog Island Oyster Company, was once the site of a large Coast Miwok settlement. The Coast Miwok left numerous oyster shell mounds around Tomales Bay, and today schoolchildren take overnight field trips to the bay and reenact aspects of Miwok culture, including a big oyster roast over a campfire.

These native populations, with an estimated eight-thousand-year history of habitation along the Pacific coast, were careful stewards of their food sources. But in 1848, when gold was discovered in California, San Francisco's population exploded and so did the demand for oysters. Accustomed to the larger, meatier Eastern oyster, newcomers gobbled up thousands of the silver-dollar-sized oysters, which, along with Champagne, enjoyed a reputation as a symbol of wealth and prestige. A robust oyster trade developed in and around San Francisco. Packed into barrels of seawater, the native oysters were delivered by pack train to the mining camps

HANGTOWN FRY

There are several stories about the origin of Hangtown fry, the famous oyster omelet. The most well-documented account appears in Joseph Conlin's book, *Bacon, Beans, and Galantines: Food and Foodways on the Western Mining Frontier.* According to Conlin, Hangtown fry may have been among the many significant contributions that Chinese immigrants made to California cuisine. The story goes that Hangtown fry was invented when a miner, his pockets filled with pouches of gold, arrived giddy and hungry in Hangtown (now Placerville), California. At the Carey House, he demanded the most expensive food available: At that time, this was eggs and oysters, both a dollar apiece. The cook was most likely Chinese, and what the miner got was an inventive egg foo yung, a staple in Cantonese cooking: an omelet incorporating fried bacon and fried oysters (see the recipe on page 136).

and towns of California and as far as Reno, 220 miles east of San Francisco, where they were sold for as much as a dollar each. Reno's Capital Chop House menu boasted, "Fresh and transplanted oysters always on hand and served at all hours in any style desired."

It wasn't long though, before oyster yields from San Francisco Bay began to decline to the point of near extinction. Part of the reason was the short-sightedness of Bay oystermen. Native oyster populations will sustain themselves if they can successfully reproduce. Free-swimming oyster larvae must have a substrate to attach themselves to, and the best material is a calcium-rich oyster shell. Profit-minded oystermen sold their shucked oyster shells to cement and poultry-feed producers, thus depriving the oyster larvae of a suitable home to grow to maturity. But the worst blow came as the result of a new form of gold mining.

By 1864, the rich surface and river deposits of gold in the Sierra Nevada foothills were exhausted, and a more invasive method of moving gold-laden soil was devised. The hillsides and riverbanks around Nevada City, California, were blasted with powerful streams of water, loosening the soil, which was then diverted into sluice boxes. Hydraulic mining became the chief means of extracting gold for the next twenty years, and it created

an environmental catastrophe. Before an injunction halted hydraulic mining in 1883, an estimated $1^1/_2$ billion cubic yards of soil and rock—eight times the amount moved to create the Panama Canal—were blasted from the Sierra hillsides and dumped into nearby creeks and rivers. The soil was carried down from the mountains by the Sacramento and San Joaquin Rivers, which in turn deposited it into San Francisco Bay. Native oyster populations in the bay plummeted as that body of water continued to fill with the washed-out sides of the foothills. Today, the remains of oyster "reefs"— clusters of millions of oysters along the fringes of the bay—are buried under layers of silt.

With demand still high, a fervent search for a new source of oysters began, and traders found it in Washington Territory in Shoalwater Bay (now called Willapa Bay). The Columbia River changed its course during the last Ice Age to meet the Pacific Ocean just to the south; before that it drained into Shoalwater Bay, creating a massive sandspit peninsula that became the perfect habitat for millions of native Western oysters. James Russell, an enterprising immigrant to the Shoalwater area, introduced San Franciscans to this new source of native Western oysters. Employing local Chinook Indians to gather the bivalves, Russell began shipping

OYSTER AQUACULTURE

Oystermen have long known that after spawning, free-swimming oyster larvae need to attach to a suitable substrate. To encourage this, growers learned to cover bay bottoms with "cultch"—gravel or discarded oyster shells—in anticipation of sets of oyster larvae attaching there and growing to harvest size. This method works well as long as nature cooperates—that is, until any of a host of undesirable conditions arise. A spike or drop in water temperature can interfere with reproduction or spawning; the larvae can be swept away by an unseasonable storm; or the "set," the stage when the larvae attach themselves to the oyster shell substrate on the bottom, might be insufficient to yield a forecasted harvest.

Innovative oystermen began to ask if it were possible to control spawning conditions to overcome the flaws and uncertainties of existing systems of cultivation. In the 1970s, in an effort to control both quality and production, the oyster hatchery was born. In the hatchery, the environment for the parent oysters (broodstock) can be carefully controlled to create ideal conditions for spawning. Oyster larvae settle out and attach to pieces of oyster shell substrate, usually held in mesh bags or other containers. After these seed oysters attach to it, this substrate, or cultch, can be transferred to oyster beds to allow the oysters to grow out to marketable size. Hatcheries allow oyster growers a measure of control over their harvests that was impossible when they relied on natural spawning.

Shortly after hatchery technology was developed, the concept of true artisanal oyster production emerged. Cultch methods, whether they use nursery-spawned or wild-spawned spat, are entirely appropriate for the end product—shucked and packaged quality oysters sold in large quantities. But the emerging market for oysters on the half-shell, freshly shucked on site at an oyster bar or restaurant, has played an important role in advancing the techniques for growing high quality half-shell oysters. Originally used in European oyster aquaculture, "single seed" or "cultchless" methods allow the oyster farmer to produce oysters much better suited for half-shell use. In the nursery, larvae attach to extremely tiny particles of finely ground oyster shell. When the spat grow to the size of small peppercorns, they are delivered to the bays and estuaries where, lovingly and laboriously tended, they will grow to marketable size in specially designed equipment that will keep them protected from predators and bathed in nutrient-rich currents that carry away their wastes and help temper their shells and their meat.

The labor that goes into growing a single artisanal oyster is far above that needed to grow an oyster using the cultch method. The economic advantage for the artisanal grower is that more spat grow to marketable size, they are worth more when they get to market, and the grower can sell them more directly without the expensive step of having them shipped to a processing plant for shucking and packing. The advantage in taste is evident to oyster lovers who relish the experience of eating a carefully raised, utterly fresh oyster right from its beautifully formed shell.

thousands of baskets of oysters to San Francisco. It was a very profitable business, not only for Russell, but for shippers and traders as well: a basket of oysters sold for a dollar in Shoalwater Bay, $30 in San Francisco's wholesale seafood markets, and $60 to the oyster-hungry public.

San Francisco entrepreneurs saw the tremendous profits being made by Washington's oyster exporters and devised a plan to rebuild the bay's oyster stocks. With the completion of the transcontinental railroad in 1869 and its western terminus in Oakland, California, on the shore of the bay, transporting oysters by rail became a viable enterprise. Oystermen began shipping juvenile Eastern oysters, primarily from New York, to be transplanted into San Francisco Bay. Up to eight thousand oysters were packed into each barrel and sold to San Francisco oyster growers for $5 per barrel. In the mild climate and warmer waters of San Francisco Bay, the oysters grew to market size in about three years—a year earlier than on the East Coast. With very little effort, an oyster grower could realize a hefty profit—that is, if his oyster beds weren't burglarized too often. (In Jack London's short story "A Raid on the Oyster Pirates," the nuances of oyster thieving on San Francisco Bay are related in colorful, hilarious detail.)

Records are incomplete on the number of shipments made during this period, but we do know that between 1887 and 1900, approximately 124 freight car loads per year (or 33,480 bushels) of baby Eastern oysters were shipped from East Coast shores to San Francisco Bay. The importation and farming of Eastern oysters made oystering California's most lucrative fishery from the late 1800s through 1910, but success came with a hefty environmental price. The invasive oyster drill snail was a menacing stowaway in those barrels of young oysters, and without natural predators, it quickly dominated the oyster beds. Oyster growers attempted to starve out the oyster drill by not replanting infested beds, but by the time of the first world war, San Francisco Bay's oyster industry had fallen victim to the same fate as the Chesapeake's: predators and industrial pollution had wiped out the productive Eastern-oyster beds as well as many other ecosystems. There was a subsequent lull in the California oyster business for about thirty-five years, until the Japanese import *Crassostrea gigas*, now called the Pacific oyster, was brought to California's waters after making its debut up the coast in Washington.

HOW *CRASSOSTREA GIGAS* CAME TO AMERICA

While San Francisco Bay oystermen tended to their established oyster beds populated with Eastern oysters, Washington state oystermen in and around Willapa Bay were taking measures to ensure the viability of the native Western oyster—now called the Olympia oyster in honor of the new state capital. Dikes were built in and around intertidal areas to keep out natural predators, facilitate harvesting, and manage oyster production. In spite of all efforts to keep the Olympia oyster market thriving, the little oyster couldn't compete with the production of the faster growing Eastern oyster. San Francisco, now well-supplied with a local source of Eastern oysters, stopped buying Olympia oysters from Washington and demand fell sharply. By the mid 1880s, the price for a sack of a thousand Olympia oysters had fallen from $16 to $2.50.

But not all was lost. With new rail lines and connections to the East Coast, Washington oyster growers soon brought in Eastern oysters and began farming them just like their San Francisco counterparts, and with a rapidly expanding population in the Pacific Northwest, they now had a local market for their product. The little Olympia oyster faded into the backdrop of an extraordinary rebound in Washington's oyster industry—one now farming almost exclusively Eastern oysters. Within ten years, at the end of the 1800s, the industry boasted $1 million in sales. By 1919, though, the entire enterprise had collapsed again. There was no single cause for the collapse. Lack of seed, overharvesting, and a toxic red tide all contributed to the Eastern oyster's demise in Washington.

The perseverence of the oyster farmer rose once again to welcome another newcomer to Washington's bays and tidelands the Japanese oyster *Crassostrea gigas*. This vigorous oyster had been farmed in Japan's waters for over four hundred years in environments similar to those of the Pacific Northwest. Hardy and fast-growing, it was able to reach sexual maturity in one year and therefore multiply rapidly. It was also more resistant to the factors that had decimated the Eastern oyster in Washington State.

Two Japanese immigrants, J. E. "Emy" Tsukimoto and Joe Miyagi, who had both been educated in Olympia, Washington, and had worked in the Willapa Bay oyster industry, seized on the idea of importing *Crassostrea gigas* seed from Japan and planting it in Puget Sound. With capital from

Seattle's Japanese community and family connections in Japan, they brought the first commercially successful Pacific oyster spat to the United States and planted it on six hundred purchased acres of Samish Bay tideland. They called their venture the Pearl Oyster Company. Sadly, The federal Anti-Alien Land Act of 1921 forced Tsukimoto and Miyagi out of the oyster-farming business. The Pearl Oyster Company was purchased by another pioneering oysterman, E. N. Steele, who continued an association with its founders. Tsukimoto and Miyagi returned to Japan and supplied Steele and others with high-quality seed.

Steele was a consummate promoter who understood that consumers are slow to accept change, so he introduced the new oyster using creative and aggressive marketing. The dark-gilled Pacific bivalve was promoted to the public with this spin: "Look for the oysters with the velvet rim." Steele traveled throughout the Northwest, putting on cooking demonstrations and encouraging retail and wholesale customers to try new oyster recipes. The University of Washington's Home Economics Department caught on, and with Steele's assistance produced a folder of recipes. The popularity of the Pacific oyster took hold, and today it is the most extensively cultivated oyster in the world.

The introduction of the Pacific oyster to North America spurred the development of more sophisticated methods of oyster aquaculture, which made it possible to farm-raise the Kumamoto oyster (another Japanese import) and the European flat.

And that brings us to the five species of oyster now cultivated and harvested in North America today: the Eastern (*Crassostrea virginica*); the native Western, or Olympia (*Ostrea conchaphila*); the Pacific (*Crassostrea gigas*); the European flat (*Ostrea edulis*); and the Kumamoto (*Crassostrea sikamea*). All oyster varieties harvested in North America—of which there are many—belong to one of these species. You'll meet many of the best-loved varieties in the next chapter.

OYSTERS' NUTRITIONAL PUNCH

High in zinc, potassium, and vitamins A, B-12, C, and D, oysters are also a great source of cholesterol-reducing omega-3 fatty acids. A $3\frac{1}{2}$-ounce serving of oysters (about 3 small oysters) contains 69 calories, 2.5 milligrams of fat, and .44 milligrams of omega-3s.

CHAPTER 2

INTRODUCING OYSTER VARIETIES

To love an oyster, it is not necessary to know its name. For most people, it is enough to tip a freshly shucked oyster into the mouth and, for a moment, be transported to that sublime place where the palate meets the sea. But to be a connoisseur of oysters—ah, that is another thing entirely. The knowledge of and ability to discern and distinguish among the species and varieties of oysters will enable you to appreciate their subtle (and sometimes not-so-subtle) differences in flavor and texture.

It's surprising to learn that there are only two species of oysters native to North America: *Crassostrea virginica*, commonly called the Eastern or Gulf oyster; and *Ostrea conchaphila*, the native oyster of the Pacific Coast, also called the Olympia oyster. Three other species were introduced to North America for farming, primarily on the West Coast: *Ostrea edulis*, the European flat oyster; *Crassostrea gigas* or Pacific oyster, the prodigious import from Japan; and *Crassostrea sikamea*, another oyster native to Japan, commonly called the Kumamoto.

So, with a total of only five species of oysters grown North America, why are there dizzying numbers of oysters with different names—like Malpeque, Willapa Bay, Blue Point, Apalachicola, Wellfleet, and Hog Island Sweetwater, to mention just a few—available for eating? With few exceptions,

As I ate the oysters with their strong taste of the sea and their faint metallic taste that the cold white wine washed away, leaving only the sea taste and the succulent texture, and as I drank their cold liquid from each shell and washed it down with the crisp taste of the wine, I lost the empty feeling and began to be happy and to make plans.

ERNEST HEMINGWAY

nearly all of the trade names for oysters, regardless of the species, are derived from the bays, estuaries, and inlets where the oysters are harvested, or the towns nearby. The exceptions to the geographic connection have snappy market names that give no indication of their origin or species. The guide that follows will help you navigate through the species, regions, and market names of nearly fifty North American oyster varieties.

To begin, generally speaking, oysters that come from the East Coast of the United States, eastern Canada, and the southern, warmer waters of the Gulf states are *Crassostrea virginica*, or Eastern oysters. A few oyster farms on the East Coast are experimenting with introduced species such as *Ostrea edulis*, the European flat oyster. Most East Coast oyster growers are reseeding natural oyster beds with hatchery-born oysters. The oysters mature, without much intervention from the oystermen, until they are harvested and sorted according to size.

On the Pacific Coast, many oyster farms employ the same growing methods as those on the East Coast—planting oyster beds from hatchery seed. But instead of farming the Eastern oyster, *Crassostrea virginica*, West Coast oyster farms plant and harvest primarily Pacific oysters, *Crassostrea gigas*. The West Coast is also home to more sophisticated methods of oyster aquaculture, employing controlled methods to produce oysters that are more consistent in shape and taste (see page 22). Hog Island Oyster Company is one of the oyster farms on the Pacific Coast to use these methods, and one result is their award-winning and wildly popular Hog Island Sweetwater, a Pacific oyster. Hog Island also farms Eastern oysters (called Atlantics at Hog Island), Kumamotos, and Manila clams.

THE NATIVE WESTERN OYSTER OR OLYMPIA (*Ostrea conchaphila*)

The little native Western oyster, *Ostrea conchaphila*, commonly called the Olympia, was harvested almost to extinction in the nineteenth century and has not been a great commercial success due to its slow growth and sensitive habitat requirements. In its natural habitat, the native Western oyster grows in tiered reefs and sometimes in "cultches"— clumps of substrate. Taylor Shellfish Farms and Olympia Oyster Company grow small quantities of Olympias at their Washington farms. Olympia oysters have a very flat and fragile shell and rarely grow bigger than the size of a silver dollar.

THE EASTERN OYSTER (*Crassostrea virginica*)

Eastern oyster shells have smooth edges, a relatively smooth top shell and a shallow bottom shell, and don't break easily. Cultivated Eastern oysters will be more uniform in shape than wild-harvested ones. Cold-water Easterns have firmer, fuller meat than their Gulf counterparts. Due to the broad geographic range of this oyster, taste can vary widely. Small Eastern oysters, especially those that are cultivated, are always best eaten raw, on the half shell. Larger ones, like those found in the Gulf, are best cooked. In the oyster trade, Eastern oysters sold in the shell are sized small, medium, and large. Smalls are 3 to 4 inches long, mediums 4 to 5 inches long, and larges 5 to 7 inches long.

THE PACIFIC OYSTER (*Crassostrea gigas*)

The Pacific oyster is one of the prettiest oysters found in North America—and one of the most widely cultivated marine organisms in the world (in North America, it's grown primarily on the West Coast). Its shell comes in colors ranging from pale green to deep purple with lengthwise stripes. Cultivating creates a deep-cupped shell, often with a sharp, fluted edge. In trade terminology, an extra-small Pacific oyster is 2 to 3 inches in length, and is almost always eaten raw. Small Pacific oysters, 3 to 4 inches long, can be eaten raw but are great for grilling, and when shucked into a stew or chowder they offer a perfect bite-sized portion. Medium Pacifics, 4 to 5 inches long, are almost exclusively used for grilling. Shucking one and popping it raw into the mouth isn't recommended unless you have something to prove—it's just too much of a good thing all at once.

THE KUMAMOTO (*Crassostrea sikamea*)

The little Kumamoto is another successful transplant from Japan, and since the first seed oyster came to the United States in 1945, Kumamotos have become one of the most sought-after oysters in North America. They are relatively small compared to the Pacific oyster, never bigger than 2 inches across, but the bottom shell is a very deep cup and filled to the brim with a sweet, tender meat. Kumis are extremely easy to shuck and are

FAMOUS CHEF EATS COWBOY

In 2005, celebrity chef Bobby Flay came to the Hog Island farm to film a segment for his Food Network show. After a grueling day of shooting, Mike Watchorn showed Bobby an unusually large oyster that the harvesting crew had found in the oyster beds. Hog Island oysters are harvested by size, and the large ones are never bigger than a small half-breast of chicken. This big oyster was a rogue, an oyster-gone-wild, a beefy anomaly—in the unique parlance of Hog Island, a cowboy.

On seeing the big 12$^1/_2$-inch-long oyster, Bobby got a second wind and, within minutes, was fanning the coals on the barbecue and getting ready to throw the cowboy on the fire. Now, most regular-size oysters will start to bubble along the seam within a few minutes. Not the cowboy. Twenty minutes over hot coals and still no sign that the big oyster was boiling inside its shell. Finally, thirty-three minutes later, Bobby, with Mike's help, pried the top shell off of the cowboy. A huge hunk of cooked oyster filled the shell—so large that they shucked it onto a carving board and sliced it up like a Sunday pot roast. Mike, Bobby, and members of the film crew feasted on the cowboy. Bobby was so delighted with the experience that he took the shell home to New York so he could show his kids the remains of the massive bivalve.

the perfect starter oyster. They are slower growing than their Pacific (*Crassostrea gigas*) cousins, but they are still good in the summer months when other oysters may be soft and spawny.

THE EUROPEAN FLAT (*Ostrea edulis*)

The European flat oyster, also known as a plate (given their flat, platelike shell), is the native oyster of the Atlantic Coast of Europe. (When grown in the area of Belon in France, *Ostrea edulis* are called Belons.) They are cultivated in the United States by only a few oyster farms, primarily in Maine, California, and Washington. Hog Island has been growing flats (called French Hogs at the farm) for eighteen years, though success came only after much trial and error—they are not nearly as hardy and resilient as Pacifics or Eastern oysters. Flats have a sweet, coppery finish that lingers for twenty minutes or more, like an afterglow. The first time I had a flat, I was hooked. The coppery flavor comes from the oyster's self-selection of minerals in its environment. This is an oyster that begs to be eaten raw and unadorned. Sadly, European flats around the world have been infected with an organism that causes adult oysters to die shortly before they reach harvest age. This protozoan parasite, *Bonamia ostrae*, quickly adapts to and pervades a marine environment, and has proven impossible to eradicate. Unless a remedy is found, European flats will be gone from oyster bar menus in a few short years. Fortunately, *Bonamia* is species-specific and does not affect any other type of oyster. It is also completely harmless to humans, and it's safe to eat the few European flats that make it to market.

WHAT OYSTERS TASTE LIKE

To the uninitiated (usually a first timer), an oyster is almost always described as salty, briny, or tasting "like the ocean." But the range of subtle flavors in oysters is as varied as the location and habitat where they grow. In the world of wines, the wonderful French word *terroir* is difficult to translate directly into English, but roughly refers to the totality of an environment and all of its attendant nuances—the soil, the air, the climate, and the characteristics of the seasons in a region. The concept of *terroir* can also be applied to a marine environment, where water temperature, tides, salinity, food sources, exposure to air and sun, and growing methods all affect the flavor of an oyster. For instance, oysters that grow near the open ocean are often saltier than those coming from estuaries that have freshwater feeder streams. Hog Island Sweetwaters are so named because the beds are ideally situated near the outlet of Walker Creek, a pure freshwater stream that balances the saltiness of the oyster liquor with a smoky sweetness. Hog Island Sweetwater oysters are slightly saltier in the drier summer months, because there is less fresh "top" water from rain flowing into the bay where the beds are located.

A corollary also exists between wine grape varieties and oyster species. Broadly speaking, in the hands of a good wine maker, wines made from Chardonnay or Pinot Noir grapes will reflect the flavor characteristics of these grape varieties. In a marine environment, two different species of oyster grown side by side, such as Pacifics and European flats, will taste vastly different in spite of the same *terroir*. Different species of oysters will self-select flavor characteristics from their environments based on what they eat and metabolize. Olympias and European flats are known for their pleasing mineral finish, because they have a higher mineral uptake—especially of copper and iodine—when they filter-feed than other oyster species. Pacific oysters are sometimes described as having a watermelon or cucumber finish, which is probably due to the types and amount of

...small and rich, looking like little ears enfolded in shells, and melting between the palate and the tongue like salted sweets.

GUY DE MAUPASSANT

microalgaes the bivalves retain after filter-feeding.

Other factors play an important role in taste, too. The amount of energy an oyster puts into reproduction results in a higher concentration of glycogen, which translates into a sweeter oyster. An algae bloom or a particularly rainy season will change the baseline flavor characteristics. The more you eat oysters, the more sensitive your palate becomes to the subtle nuances of oyster flavors. Try eating your favorite oysters year-round to experience the full range of flavor differentiators. You'll notice that your favorite oyster will taste different in the middle of winter than it does in early fall. The texture of the meat may be softer during warmer months and firmer during cold weather. Keep a journal of oyster tasting notes alongside notations on rainfall and temperature—you might find a pattern.

But like all things sensual, flavors are inherently subjective. The tasting guide below is just a beginning and gives you the broad categories of flavor and texture—a reference point from which to start exploring.

As an oyster-lover, I have experienced many different flavor characteristics, including melon, lettuce, cucumber, citrus, and an aftertaste that's smoky, coppery, and metallic. At the end of the day, however, I can't dismiss the wisdom of a friendly, big-hearted Canadian oysterman I once interviewed. When I asked him if he thought his oysters had a "melon finish," as some food reviewers had stated, he paused, then said, "Ya know, when it comes right down to it, I think oysters taste, well, like oysters."

TASTING GUIDE

I've listed the most common terms for oysters' taste and texture characteristics below, along with relevant information on location.

A reference to the meatiness of the oyster or its texture means that this is a consistent and notable quality in a given variety.

AFTERTASTE	Lingering flavor.
BRINE/BRINY	Seawater saltiness. More complex than straight salt.
BUTTERY	Creamy, smooth, and slightly sweet.
CLEAN	Refreshing in the mouth.
CRISP	Zesty, as in fresh lemon.
FINISH	Brief aftertaste; does not linger.
FULL FLAVORED	Full, round, pleasing oyster taste.
MELON	Sweetness, as in a piece of fresh watermelon or honeydew.
MILD	No prominent flavor; balanced, slightly bland.
MINERAL	Usually copper; sometimes granite. Can be a forward taste, but is always a lingering aftertaste.
SALTY	Forward salt taste.
SMOKY	Earthy sweetness; complex, subtle, and brief.
SWEET	A sweetness analogous to tasting freshwater after saltwater.

The oyster varieties in the list that follows are among those most commonly found on oyster bar and restaurant menus. Most are varieties of Eastern and Pacific oysters, which are the most widely available. I've included notes on the other three species as well. There are, of course, other varieties and I encourage you to try these and make your own tasting notes. Similarly, strike up a conversation with your server, fishmonger, or chef to discover other varieties they have tried and enjoyed.

APALACHICOLA (Eastern oyster; *Crassostrea virginica*): Apalachicola, Florida, on the Gulf Coast. Soft meat, slightly sweet, and mild.

BEAUSOLEIL (Eastern oyster; *Crassostrea virginica*): New Brunswick, Canada. Cold Atlantic waters make this oyster briny and refreshing, with a firm texture.

BLUE POINT (Eastern oyster; *Crassostrea virginica*): Connecticut and the Long Island Sound. Has a characteristic mild Eastern flavor, with a meaty texture. Once a trade name, but now many oysters from this area are called "Blue Points."

BRAS D'OR (Eastern oyster; *Crassostrea virginica*): Nova Scotia, Canada. Over-wintered beneath the ice off Cape Breton, it takes three to four years before these briny, clean-finishing oysters reach marketable size.

CAPE BRETON (Eastern oyster; *Crassostrea virginica*): Prince Edward Island (PEI), Canada. Cold waters and slow growth give this mild oyster a sweetness, balanced with crisp brine.

CARAQUET (Eastern oyster; *Crassostrea virginica*): New Brunswick, Canada. Briny, plump, and buttery with a very firm texture.

CHESAPEAKE (Eastern oyster; *Crassostrea virginica*): The famed Chesapeake Bay oyster, with fisheries mainly in Virginia and Maryland. With both fresh- and saltwater influences, this oyster is mild and slightly sweet.

Eastern oysters (*Crassostrea virginica*)

European flats (*Ostrea edulis*)

CHILMARK (Eastern oyster; *Crassostrea virginica*): Martha's Vineyard, Massachusetts. Small to medium, with a balance of mild sweetness and salty ocean flavor.

CHINCOTEAGUE (Eastern oyster; *Crassostrea virginica*): Chincoteague Bay, Virginia and Maryland. Salty and plump, with a distinctive aftertaste.

COCKENOE (Eastern oyster; *Crassostrea virginica*): Connecticut and Long Island Sound. Moderately salty and plump, with a slight but pleasing metallic finish.

COTUIT (Eastern oyster; *Crassostrea virginica*): Cotuit Bay, Massachusetts. Plump and meaty; mildly salty, with crisp notes.

DABOB BAY (Pacific oyster; *Crassostrea gigas*): Dabob Bay (northern Hood Canal), Washington. Harvested small for half-shell eating; fresh and sweet with a slightly fruity aftertaste.

DRAKES BAY (Pacific oyster; *Crassostrea gigas*): Drakes Bay, Point Reyes Peninsula, California. Pristine estuary waters make this oyster clean, fresh, and mildly salty.

EMERALD COVE (Pacific oyster; *Crassostrea gigas*): Baynes Sound, British Columbia, Canada. Tray-cultured, with sweet, plump meat. Harvested small for half-shell eating.

EUROPEAN FLAT (French flat, plate; *Ostrea edulis*): Washington State, Tomales Bay, California, and Maine. A beautiful flat shell, with a copper-colored oyster inside. Sweet, with a strong copper finish. Same species as the famous Belon oysters from France. Because they're susceptible to a species-specific parasite (harmless to humans), they are rare in North America.

FANNY BAY (Pacific oyster; *Crassostrea gigas*): Fanny Bay, British Columbia, Canada. Very salty and sweet, often with a cucumber or melon finish. Plump and meaty.

GALVESTON BAY (Eastern oyster; *Crassostrea virginica*): Galveston Bay, Texas. Big shells, with very mild meat and brine; sometimes has a metallic aftertaste.

GLIDDEN POINT (Eastern oyster; *Crassostrea virginica*): Damariscotta River estuary, Maine. Clean, fresh, and briny, with a firm, meaty texture.

GOLDEN MANTLE (Pacific oyster; *Crassostrea gigas*): Sunshine Coast, British Columbia, Canada. Mild and sweet, with a watermelon finish.

HAMA HAMA (Pacific oyster; *Crassostrea gigas*): Hama Hama River Delta (Hood Canal), Washington. Briny, with a mild finish and consistently firm meat.

HOG ISLAND ATLANTIC (Eastern oyster; *Crassostrea virginica*): Tomales Bay, California. Mildly briny; very crisp, with a subtle mineral (granite) finish.

HOG ISLAND SWEETWATER (Pacific oyster; *Crassostrea gigas*): Tomales Bay, California. Deeply cupped, plump, and sweet. Has a well-balanced saltiness, with a smoky finish.

INDIAN RIVER (Eastern oyster; *Crassostrea virginica*): Indian River Lagoon (Atlantic Coast), Florida. A prominent seawater flavor; briny.

KUMAMOTO (Kumamoto oyster; *Crassostrea sikamea*): California, Oregon, Washington. Juicy, sweet, and buttery, with a smooth melon finish. A great choice for first-time oyster eaters.

KUSSHI (Pacific oyster; *Crassostrea gigas*): Deep Bay, British Columbia, Canada. Very mild, with a hint of brininess and a soft cucumber finish.

LOUISIANA GULF (Eastern oyster; *Crassostrea virginica*): Mississippi River bayous, Louisiana. A soft texture and very plump and mild, with a slightly salty and abundant liquor. Eat raw during coldwater harvest only. Eating Gulf oysters is not recommended from April through October, when warmer waters cause bacteria levels to rise (see page 54).

MALASPINA (Pacific oyster; *Crassostrea gigas*): Malaspina Sound, Vancouver Island, Canada. Plump and hearty, with a mild, sweet finish.

Kumamotos (*Crassostrea sikamea*)

Olympias (*Ostrea conchaphila*)

MALPEQUE (Eastern oyster; *Crassostrea virginica*): Prince Edward Island (PEI), Canada. A smooth texture; buttery, with a well-balanced salty-sweet liquor.

MOHEGAN (Eastern oyster; *Crassostrea virginica*): Wamphassuc Point, Connecticut. Sustainably farmed by the Mohegan tribe. Plump, juicy, slightly salty, and full flavored, with a clean finish.

MOONSTONE (Eastern oyster; *Crassostrea virginica*): Narragansett, Rhode Island. A distinct and full-bodied oyster flavor; briny, with a meaty texture.

OLYMPIA (Native Pacific oyster; *Ostrea conchaphila*): Washington and California. Rare, because difficult to farm. Small in size, with a round, flat shell. Has a slightly sweet and robust burst of flavor, with a pleasing coppery aftertaste.

PEARL POINT (Pacific oyster; *Crassostrea gigas*): Netarts Bay, Oregon. A clean and crisp flavor, a firm texture, and a well-balanced finish.

PENN COVE (Pacific oyster; *Crassostrea gigas*): Puget Sound, Washington. Crisp and briny, with a clean and refreshing aftertaste.

PICKLE POINT (Eastern oyster; *Crassostrea virginica*): Prince Edward Island (PEI), Canada. Salty and crisp, with a firm texture and a sweet aftertaste.

PINE ISLAND (Eastern oyster; *Crassostrea virginica*): Oyster Bay Harbor, Long Island, New York. Mild and sweet, though saltier than most Atlantic coast oysters.

QUILCENE (Pacific oyster; *Crassostrea gigas*): northern Hood Canal, Washington. A delicate texture, with a medium salty-sweet finish.

SINKU (Pacific oyster; *Crassostrea gigas*): British Columbia, Canada. Very crisp and clean, with a melon finish and delicate meat.

SISTER POINT (Pacific oyster; *Crassostrea gigas*): southern Hood Canal, Washington. Deeply cupped, with a meaty texture and a mildly briny, sweet finish.

SKOOKUM INLET (Pacific oysters; *Crassostrea gigas*): Puget Sound, Washington. Smoky sweet, with a mild aftertaste and a plump texture.

SNOW CREEK (Pacific oyster; *Crassostrea gigas*): Discovery Bay, Olympic Peninsula, Washington. A crisp ocean flavor; medium brine, with a sweet finish.

STELLAR BAY (Pacific oyster; *Crassostrea gigas*): Cortes Island, British Columbia, Canada. Salty and mildly sweet, with a melon aftertaste.

SUMMER ICE (Pacific oyster; *Crassostrea gigas*): British Columbia, Canada. Deep-water grown. A firm texture, mild salt, and a very clean finish.

TATAMAGOUCHE (Eastern oyster; *Crassostrea virginica*): Nova Scotia, Canada. A full oyster flavor; salty, with a firm texture.

TOMAHAWK (Eastern oyster; *Crassostrea virginica*): Martha's Vineyard, Massachusetts. Sustainably farmed by the Wampanoag tribe. Mild and briny; plump, with a smoky finish.

TOTTEN INLET (Pacific oyster; *Crassostrea gigas*): Southern Puget Sound, Washington. Briny and slightly sweet; plump and full flavored.

WELLFLEET (Eastern oyster; *Crassostrea virginica*): Cape Cod, Massachusetts. Sets the standard for Eastern oyster flavor; crisp with a smooth texture, a well-balanced brine, and firm meat.

WESTCOTT BAY (Pacific oyster; *Crassostrea gigas*): San Juan Island, Washington. Petite and plump, with well-balanced brine and a slightly sweet finish.

WILLAPA BAY (Pacific oyster; *Crassostrea gigas*): Willapa Bay, Washington. Crisp, salty, and plump, with a watermelon aftertaste.

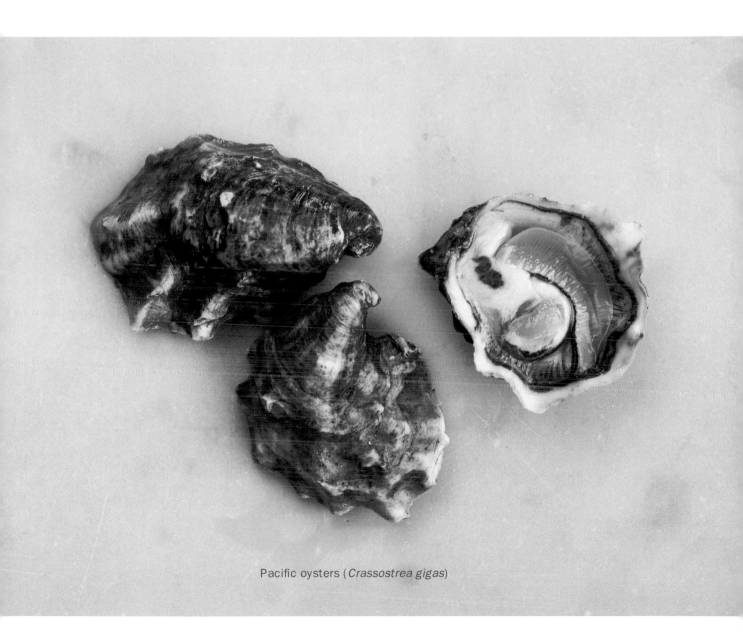

Pacific oysters (*Crassostrea gigas*)

CHAPTER 3

BUYING, HANDLING, AND ENJOYING OYSTERS

Ready for your personal oyster feast? Everything you need to know is right here—from where to buy fresh oysters in the shell to the easiest and safest method for shucking. Tips on transporting, handling, and storing oysters will make you an oyster expert in your own kitchen. If you're going out to an oyster bar or a restaurant that serves oysters, learn what you need to know about ordering and eating. And whether you're at home or bellied up to the oyster bar, this chapter will help you learn to confidently pair oysters with wines and beers.

BUYING OYSTERS IN THE SHELL

The best place to buy oysters in the shell is directly from the source: at the farm where they are cultured or harvested. If you're fortunate enough to live near a coastal oyster-growing region, then a day trip to the farm will be a rewarding experience. If not, then adding an oyster farm visit to your coastal vacation itinerary is worth the extra planning. (Most oyster-growing operations have on-site retail sales, although hours may be limited due to weather, season, and staffing, so be sure to call ahead.) If you've ever stopped at a roadside produce stand and bought corn, peaches, or berries straight from the fields behind the stand, then you know how comforting and complete it feels to buy food at the place where it's grown. Visiting an oyster farm is a wholly sensual experience that delivers a side benefit to getting the freshest possible oysters: the ambiance. You'll smell and feel the crisp, moisture-laden estuarine air, rest your eyes on the expanse of the water where the oysters grow, experience the cycle of the tides so vital to an oyster's life. If you look carefully, you'll see an entire ecosystem working in harmony: birds, sea mammals, estuary plant life, and of course, oysters. A farm visit will bring you full circle and allow you to expand your love of oysters to include the entire gestalt of the marine environment.

Hog Island runs its retail sales from the Hog Shack, a tiny building on the edge of Tomales Bay and right next to the tanks and sorting tables where workers process oysters for wholesale and retail in-the-shell sales. The staff is always happy to answer questions about Hog Island oysters, and you'll have the chance to see where the oysters are brought when they come from the bay.

Hog Island sells their oysters by species (Pacific, Eastern, or Kumamoto), by size (extra-small, small, medium), and by the dozen or the bushel (120 oysters). Most farms sell their oysters similarly, although the inventory will vary—not all farms cultivate or harvest the same species of oysters.

Since most farms are situated in pristine natural environments, you're likely to find a beautiful picnic spot nearby to enjoy your lusciously fresh oysters. Come prepared to enjoy your oysters bayside or nearby. Either on the way to your nearby oyster farm or in

a community nearby, you're bound to find food to go with your oysters. For example, visitors to Hog Island often bring wine, beer, cheese, bread, and olives to complement their oysters.

If you plan to bring your farm-bought oysters home, be sure to keep them cold, cold, cold (don't freeze them to death, though—45°F is ideal). Take a cooler with you and buy two bags of ice. Place your oysters (in the bag they come in) between the bags of ice. Don't open the bags of ice and pour them into the cooler and then place loose oysters on top. This is fine for half-shell service, but too long in a cooler and the oysters will die in the freshwater ice melt. If you find yourself unprepared, buy a small Styrofoam cooler and ice. In a pinch, a cardboard box, two bags of ice, and some towels will suffice if your trip home doesn't last more than a couple of hours. Never, never leave your oysters in a warm car without ice. Don't be fooled by the shells—they act more like heat incubators than protective insulators. When they heat up, they will hold that heat and you'll end up with dead oysters and invite bacterial growth and, quite possibly, food-borne illness. Treat fresh, live oysters with the same care as you would fresh fish and fresh meat.

If you can't make it to an oyster farm, the second best way to buy fresh oysters in the shell is to visit your local fishmonger or upscale grocery store. Both deal with seafood brokers and distributors, and if they don't routinely stock fresh oysters, you may be able to special-order them.

If you see oysters in the seafood case, make sure they're on ice—oysters should be stored just like any other fresh seafood. Every state has an agency that mandates that growers and harvesters must attach a shellfish tag to every bag or box of oysters. The tag tells buyers, at a minimum, the date the oysters were harvested, the date they were shipped, and the area where they were harvested. These tags must remain attached to the container until it is empty. While the tag doesn't guarantee food safety, it's comforting to know that these strict regulations are in place. In most states, the tag must be displayed in the case. If it is not, ask the seafood manager if you can see the tag and look for the date harvested, the source, and the date shipped.

Don't buy any oysters that are more than five days from harvest. They may not be spoiled, but the longer oysters are out of the water, the more brine or liquor they lose, making them dry. I often tap my refrigerated oysters with the handle of my oyster knife to listen for a dull, hollow sound, which would indicate that the oyster is no longer alive, and has shrunken inside the shell and lost its liquor. If they sound empty, I toss them. With experience, you may even be able to tell a fresh oyster just by the weight of it, much like buying an orange: you can feel the juice in a good one and sense the dryness in another just by holding it in your hand.

You can also search online for a particular variety of oyster and then contact a supplier equipped to ship oysters directly to your door. Hog Island ships thousands of oysters this way. The oysters come directly out of the seawater holding tanks and into Styrofoam boxes fitted inside a waxed shipping box. Frozen gel packs keep the oysters cold during their overnight shipment. If you're able to contact a farm directly and find out that they don't ship retail, ask them to tell you where their oysters are sold in your area.

TRUE OR FALSE? ALL ABOUT THE "R"

There are many misconceptions about eating oysters or not eating oysters in months without an "R"—May, June, July, and August. The facts and exposed myths are below.

TRUE: It is not safe to eat raw, unprocessed oysters from the Gulf of Mexico during months without the letter "R," as well as April, September, and October. Period. The reason is the two bacteria, *Vibrio vulnificus* and *Vibrio parahaemolyticus*, that proliferate in warm Gulf water beginning in April and continuing through the month of October. "Processing," or pasteurization, means that the oyster has gone through a pasteurization process that destroys any harmful bacteria. The pasteurization can happen directly in the shell; although the processed oyster is no longer alive, it can be safely eaten out of the shell.

TRUE: *Vibrio vulnificus* and *Vibrio parahaemolyticus* are in the same family as cholera bacteria.

TRUE: You can safely eat raw oysters from Pacific coastal waters from northern California all the way north to Alaska year-round. There has never been a documented case of *Vibrio vulnificus* from West Coast oysters, and the waters are generally too cold for

Vibrio parahaemolyticus. Oysters from the northernmost regions of the East Coast (north of Boston), where the water is very cold, are also safe to eat year-round.

FALSE: Both *Vibrio parahaemolyticus* and *Vibrio vulnificus* cause the same flulike symptoms. What's true: *Vibrio parahaemolyticus* causes mild to severe abdominal cramping, diarrhea, nausea, vomiting, and in some cases fever and chills. Individuals with weakened immune systems will experience more severe symptoms, but *Vibrio parahaemolyticus* is rarely fatal.

Vibrio vulnificus can cause a much more serious illness. In healthy individuals, *Vibrio vulnificus* may cause the same gastrointestinal symptoms as a moderate to severe infection from *Vibrio parahaemolyticus*. People with certain pre-existing medical conditions, especially liver disease or a weakened immune system, are 80 percent more likely than healthy people to develop bloodstream infections, and without aggressive antibiotic treatment, these infections are fatal 50 percent of the time. Every reported case of *Vibrio vulnificus* has come from the Gulf States. The Centers for Disease Control posts thorough information on both *Vibrio* bacteria on its website, www. cdc.gov. Search for "vibrio."

FALSE: *Vibrio vulnificus* and *Vibrio parahaemolyticus* bacteria are caused by pollution. What's true: These are both naturally occurring marine bacteria that don't affect the oysters they inhabit.

FALSE: You can tell if an oyster is contaminated with *Vibrio parahaemolyticus* or *Vibrio vulnificus*. What's true: There's no distinctive taste, odor, or change in the look of an oyster contaminated by these bacteria.

FALSE: Modern refrigeration prevents the growth of *Vibrio vulnificus* and *Vibrio parahaemolyticus* in raw oysters. What's true: Refrigeration only slows the growth of bacteria already present. Only cooking or pasteurization can destroy *Vibrio parahaemolyticus* and *Vibrio vulnificus*.

FALSE: Oysters pasteurized in the shell taste radically different from freshly shucked live oysters. What's true: There is a slight variation in flavor—say, the difference in taste between a freshly picked apple and one that's been in cold storage for a while.

FALSE: Oysters that are spawning and soft can make you sick. What's true: Spawny oysters simply contain high concentrations of reproductive matter, which is harmless. They are considered a delicacy by some.

HANDLING AND STORAGE

The single most important thing to remember when handling fresh in-the-shell oysters is to keep them at 55°F or lower—preferably in the range below 45°F but above 35°F. At 65°F and above, bacteria will start to multiply. When you get your oysters home, wash any mud or grit from the shells under cold running water. Cleaning them in this way means that when it comes time to shuck the oysters, you won't be pushing mud into the oyster with your oyster knife. If you notice any oysters that are open, tap on the shell and see if they snap closed. If they don't respond, throw them away.

To store your oysters, take a close look at one and see which side has a flatter top shell and which has a cupped bottom shell. Eastern oysters are subtly cupped, while Pacifics and Kumamotos have a more pronounced cup. This cup is like a little pool of saltwater for the oyster and helps keep it alive and fresh. When storing oysters, always store them cupped side down. I use a rimmed baking sheet; a large, shallow casserole dish or lasagna pan works well too. I line them up until the bottom layer is full, and if I have more, I simply stack the others on top, cupped side down. Take a clean kitchen towel, wet it thoroughly and wring it out, and cover your oysters with it. Place them in the refrigerator at a temperature of 35° to 45°F (the middle rack is best). Never put oysters-in-the-shell in a sealed plastic container or cover them with plastic wrap, because oysters need to breathe.

If you bought your oysters directly from the farm, you should eat them within four or five days of purchase. Buying them from a seafood case in a grocery store means they've been out of the water longer than farm-bought ones, so you will probably need to shuck and eat them within one to two days of purchase (remember to look at the shellfish tag that tells you when they were harvested).

HOW TO ORDER AND EAT OYSTERS IN RESTAURANTS

Most restaurants purchase oysters from seafood or specialty shellfish distributors, who buy the oysters from growers. Some restaurants, however, buy direct from growers like Hog Island Oyster Company and maintain a close relationship with the farm. No matter how the restaurant gets its oysters, make sure it has a good reputation for serving fresh, high-quality foods. Most illnesses contracted from eating oysters are due to mishandling rather than infected oysters.

From the time the oysters leave the farm, they should be kept at a constant 45°F and refrigerated as soon as they arrive at a restaurant. Again, most oysters should be eaten within four to five days of leaving the water (seven at the most, if they have been consistently and appropriately refrigerated), but the best restaurants order only enough for a day or two, then get a fresh shipment.

Ordering raw oysters in a restaurant is a little like ordering wine. You'll want to know two things: where the oysters come from and how they will taste. Most oyster bars and high-end restaurants list their oysters either by their variety name or by where they were grown (which is often one and the same), or by the species name, such as Pacific, Eastern, Kumamoto, or European flat.

You will occasionally find a well-meaning restaurant that gets their oysters confused. I once found an oyster po' boy sandwich listed on the menu of a little California bistro. The menu description boasted that they used only the "freshest Pacific Blue Point oysters." Diplomatically, I pointed out to my waiter that there was no such thing as a Pacific Blue Point oyster. I explained that Blue Points come from Long Island and are a variety of the Eastern species, taste very dif-

ferent, and don't cook as well as Pacific oysters. He passed this information on to the kitchen, and shortly, the waiter and three of the kitchen staff ended up at my table with their container of fresh, already-shucked Pacific oysters, eager to learn more. I obliged happily, and now they probably know more about oysters than they wanted to.

Most restaurants that serve oysters on the half shell will be better informed than that little bistro, especially oyster bars. When the menu lists oysters by species, such as Pacific, Eastern, or Kumamoto, ask where each variety is grown. Part of the fun of eating oysters is to try a few different kinds and compare tastes. If you try a Hog Island Sweetwater, a Hama Hama, and a Fanny Bay, all Pacific oysters, you'll discover the Hama Hama is slightly saltier than the Sweetwater, and the Fanny Bay does not have the Sweetwater's soft, smoky aftertaste.

How many raw oysters you order will depend on the size of the oyster and on your appetite. A good rule of thumb is six extra-small oysters (shells 2 to 3 inches long) per person as an appetizer, and one or two dozen as a main course. It's common to see customers at the Hog Island Oyster Bar down a dozen and a half Sweetwaters and consider it a meal. Eastern and Pacific oysters are best eaten raw when they are 2 to 4 inches

in length—any bigger and it's just too much raw oyster in the mouth. Kumamoto oysters rarely get more than 1 1/2 inches in length, so you'll always get the right size.

Now that you've ordered, there's the question of whether to eat them with or without an accompaniment. Die-hards like their raw oysters completely unadorned. Good oysters eaten without condiments deliver the most intense, pure, and essential qualities of the sea. If you've never tried an oyster without a topping, give it a shot. If you want an accompaniment, what you'll usually find on restaurant and oyster bar menus is a vinegar-shallot mignonette, a cocktail sauce, fresh lemon juice, or Tabasco sauce. To make spectacular raw-oyster toppings of your own, see the recipes that begin on page 84.

Larger Pacific oysters make the best hot appetizers. Toppings can vary from a simple mignonette to the classic rich topping used for oysters Rockefeller. Hot oyster appetizers are most commonly served by the half dozen, which, depending on the richness of the sauce and topping, will satisfy two or three people.

Oyster bars, like sushi bars, give you an up-front and personal experience with the staff. At many oyster bars throughout the country, you can sit at the bar and watch while your oysters are shucked. You wouldn't think of interacting with a cook in a restaurant's open kitchen, but a good oyster shucker will answer your questions and still maintain the steady rhythm of shucking required to keep up with his orders. At the Hog Island Oyster Bar in San Francisco, the shuckers are the show, and part of their job is to speak to people at the bar. Don't be shy about talking to a shucker—you'll be doing him a favor by breaking up the monotony of shucking, and you'll learn more about oysters in the process.

Whether at a table or a bar, you'll want to know some basic oyster etiquette. Most raw oysters on the half shell are served on a platter of crushed ice, with condiments and lemon wedges. If you'd like to add condiments, scatter a teaspoon or so of the mignonette sauce, or a squirt of Tabasco or lemon over the top of an oyster, just enough to enhance the oyster's taste. Don't use more than one accompaniment at a time, because you'll bury the flavor of the oyster. You are then faced with the dilemma of using the shellfish fork or slurping the oyster right out of the shell.

The best advice is to forego the dainty fork and tip the oyster straight into your mouth. The oyster will taste much better when you include its briny liquor, and you won't offend anyone. Pick up the shell with the broad end facing toward you. With the same hand, place your index finger just slightly inside the narrow end of the shell, next to the oyster. Now, open your mouth and give the oyster a little nudge with your finger. If the oyster has been properly shucked, it will slide right into your mouth, along with the liquor. If it doesn't slide instantly out of the shell, then use your fork to release it from its shell and pop it into your mouth. When you're finished, place the shell back on the platter face down. The Hog Island guys use this ritual to as a way to step back and take a moment to appreciate the beauty of the oyster shell and the hard work of the oyster farmer.

Some restaurants and oyster bars serve oyster shooters, which are simply oysters in shot glasses accompanied by a peppery condiment, plus vodka or tequila. This is a novel way to get your oyster, but be sure to ask if the oysters are fresh, right out of the shell. If not, your oyster could come from a jar. That's probably okay, but it won't taste as good as a freshly shucked one.

TO CHEW OR NOT TO CHEW

Personally, I don't chew raw oysters. When I first ate one, a gorgeous French man just tipped my head back, pushed the oyster in my mouth, and instructed me to swallow. The sensation of the whole oyster sliding down my throat is part of the experience for me. But there are many who insist that the only way to savor an oyster is to chew it and chew it well. Hog Island cofounder John Finger is a chewer. He claims that chewing releases the complexity of flavors in the oyster. You won't know which way you like it best until you try both.

HOW TO SHUCK AN OYSTER

Opening an oyster is a conundrum. Encased inside its shell, the oyster will tighten the screws when handled. This presents a frustrating challenge to the uninitiated, but with the right technique you'll soon feel confident enough to safely shuck dozens. Before you learn how to shuck with a knife, however, you need a tour of the oyster's outer architecture and interior design. Once you understand how the oyster is constructed, deconstructing it will make a lot more sense. If you have some oysters that need to be shucked right

No, I do not weep at the world—
I am too busy sharpening my oyster knife.

ZORA NEALE HURSTON

this minute, then skip to the step-by-step instructions (see "Shucking Down" page 65) and read the details later.

The word oyster comes from the Indo-European *ost*, meaning "bone," probably due to its hefty, sometimes bone-colored shell. Oysters are members of a vast and diverse phylum of the animal kingdom, mollusks or molluscs (the Latin root of mollusk is *mollis*, meaning "soft"). In addition to their familiar relatives abalone, clams, mussels, and scallops, oysters are also related to squid and octopuses—mollusks turned inside out.

Oysters begin "laying down," or growing, shell when they are the size of tiny pepper grains. The shell is composed mainly of calcium carbonate, a hard-as-rocks material that is nearly impenetrable to predators. The two-part shell is held together by complementary mechanics: a powerful adductor muscle that pulls the top and bottom shells closed when the oyster is finished feeding or when it's tapped or otherwise molested, and

a ligament at the hinge that works in opposition to the adductor muscle. The first step to getting inside is to get past the hinge, gaining access to the place where the adductor muscle attaches to the flat top shell. Once you detach the top of the adductor muscle from the top shell, you'll get your first view of the prize: a plump, silvery morsel resting in a filtered seawater bath.

To completely liberate the oyster, you'll need to detach the adductor muscle from the cupped bottom shell. The surest indication of a novice shucker is leaving the adductor muscle attached to the bottom shell, subjecting the unwary oyster slurper to the humiliation of Badly Shucked Oyster Syndrome—a cascade of oyster liquor down the chin and a still-attached oyster dangling in front of the open mouth.

Before you get started, know your oyster species (see pages 31 to 36) and use the species-specific tips that follow for more successful shucking.

HOW HOG ISLAND GROWS PERFECT OYSTERS

An oyster-growing colleague who had just returned to California from Down Under stopped by Hog Island one day in the early nineties and said "Hey guys, check this out . . . it's a cradle for baby oysters." He handed them a brochure on a product called a Stanway, a three-foot-long cylinder of plastic mesh with foam caps on each end, about the size of a bed bolster. The Aussies were using Stanways to cradle their baby oysters as a way to coax them into forming deeper-cupped shells. John and Mike said, "What the heck," and ordered one hundred. Since then, they've had so much success with the Stanway that every baby Pacific oyster is gently rocked for its first six months on the farm. Here's how it works.

The baby oysters (spat) arrive from the hatchery about ¼ inch long, and with a tiny, newly formed hinge curving down and away from the top shell like a hook. If left to grow unattended, the hinge would stay in that position and the bottom shell would naturally form a shallow cup. But at Hog Island, about twenty-five hundred spat go straight into each Stanway, which is submerged in the nutrient-rich waters of Tomales Bay and tethered to keep it from being washed out to sea. As the tides ebb and flow, the oyster cradle is rocked by the current and gently tumbles the spat. The repetitive tumbling causes the bill of the shell (the broad end opposite the hinge) to erode slightly, stimulating the spat to lay down more shell from the hinge. Eventually, the bottom shell becomes more deeply cupped and the hinge begins to flatten out along the top shell. (The flatter hinge makes the oysters easier to shuck.) At six months, the architecture of the shell is established and the spat are moved from the Stanway to the grow-out area, where they are placed in flat mesh bags.

After one to two years, depending on how fast each individual grows, the oysters are harvested, and what perfectly beautiful oysters they are: deeply cupped and uniform, with the highly articulated fluting characteristic of the Pacific oyster. But the lovely shell is not all for show. As the deep cups forms, it reduces the length of the bill, making a bigger home for the oyster to grow into. The larger cup also accommodates more seawater, which keeps the oyster healthy and happy.

After harvesting, Hog Island takes a few more steps to make sure their oysters stay safe and in top condition. First, the oysters are removed from their mesh bags, sorted, graded by size, and hosed off to remove any debris. Then every oyster is submerged in a seawater tank system for 1 to 2 days. The water in the tanks comes from the bay but before it enters the tanks, it is filtered through an ultraviolet light sterilizer to kill any harmful bacteria, then through a water-chiller that drops the temperature below 50°F. The UV sterilizer and the cold water filter ensure that no bacterial growth can occur before the oysters are shipped or sold.

Letting the oysters rest in cold seawater postharvest has other benefits. Harvesting exposes the oysters to stress, and as lovingly as they are handled by the crew, they need some time to recover. The tank system is like a little spa for the oysters, where they can rest and purge any particulate matter still inside their shells. All Hog Island oysters go straight from the tanks into the hands of customers or onto refrigerated trucks for transport—clean, rested, and with a seawater (rather than a refrigerator) chill in their flesh.

Pacific Oysters

Pacific oysters (*Crassostrea gigas*) are grown either loose, on the bottoms of bays or estuaries, or in suspended trays or bags. How they grow profoundly affects the way the shell is formed. Where oysters are cultivated by seeding former oyster beds or gravelly intertidal beaches, the shells are less uniform and less fluted than those grown by suspension, and this makes shucking a little trickier. All the external parts of the shell are easily located, but the hinge shape varies. Just like belly buttons, oyster hinges can be innies and outies and everything in between. The hinge may have formed in a curved-down position, so you may have to position the oyster at different angles when you start to shuck. The edges of the shell may be dulled from being rolled and tossed on the beach or bottom by tidal movements and

A Find the sweet spot.

B Wiggle the knife to pop the hinge.

C Rotate the oyster and slide the knife in and back along the top shell to cut the top adductor muscle.

D The top adductor is cut cleanly and the top shell is off (you can see on the shell where the top adductor was attached).

E Slide the knife under the oyster to detach the bottom adductor muscle and free the oyster in its shell.

the hinge area, letting the knife do the work, not your hand. Apply some pressure to your wiggling. The goal is to find the sweet spot on the hinge and smoothly slip the knife point in without cracking off shell. (Picture B.)

7. You'll know you're "in" when you feel a release in pressure and the knife slips incrementally into the oyster. Using a twisting motion, "pop" the top shell. *Stop.* Withdraw your knife and, still holding it in your right hand, wipe the end off on the towel to avoid inserting any mud or shell into the oyster on your next move.

8. In one motion, reinsert the knife into the oyster, keeping the blade angled up and away from you along the inside of the top shell, and scrape the adductor muscle off the top shell, taking care not to cut into the oyster meat. (Picture C.) With a slight twist of your wrist and help from your left hand, the top shell will fold over and off. (Picture D.)

9. Now, flip the opened oyster around on the towel so that the hinge is facing to the left. Be careful not to spill any of the liquor. Wipe the tip of your knife off again and gently hold the oyster with your gloved hand. Using the knife tip, pick off any broken shell or debris that you find around the outer edge of the bottom shell.

10. While still holding the shell with your gloved hand, locate the adductor muscle where it attaches to the shell—on most oysters the muscle will be along the edge of the shell closest to you. In one fluid stroke, angle your knife down and away from you and cut through the bottom adductor muscle. (Picture E.)

Success means that you haven't hacked the oyster meat and it is still intact.

Shucking In-Hand

Shucking an oyster while holding it in one hand is for experienced oyster shuckers only. Don't try this until you've completely mastered shucking down. Showing off before you're ready to shuck in-hand is a dangerous proposition. Just ask my brother-in-law, Ron Parisi. He had the shucking down method mastered and thought he'd try to shuck in-hand. We heard a small shriek and turned around to find Ron with a long-blade oyster knife poking out the top of his hand between his ring and middle fingers. Thankfully, the knife missed a tendon, but he was bandaged up for weeks, depriving him of his daily surfing sessions. Bummer.

You will need: a left-handed leather-palmed glove (an old cycling glove works great), a protective rubberized glove (see page 72), also for your left hand, a 4-inch-blade oyster knife, and a kitchen towel. Note: these instructions are for right-handers. Left-handers, reverse positions (put the gloves on your right hand, take the knife in your left, and so on).

1. Put the leather-palmed glove on your left hand, then put the rubberized glove over it. Place the folded towel on a work surface.

2. Stand facing the work surface and grasp the oyster in your left hand, firmly wrapping your fingers around the edges—this will help match the force of your knife hand. Your hand should be at a 45-degree angle from your body.

3. Insert the knife point into the hinge. The knife should be on the same plane as the top shell. (Picture A.)

4. Keeping the knife somewhat stationary, and with a steady pressure, begin to wiggle the oyster into the knife point—this settles the knife into the "sweet spot." Then, by using a combination of short side-to-side wiggles of the oyster together with the knife, you'll be able to "pop" the hinge. (Picture B.) Be sure to maintain your arms and hands at a 45-degree angle to your body—this helps you have more control (the tendency is to raise your arms as you exert increased force).

5. Next, rotate the oyster, while at the same time sliding the knife farther under the top shell, cutting through the top adductor muscle. (Picture C.)

6. Remove the flat top shell. Turn the oyster around in your left hand so that the hinge is facing you. Slide the knife carefully under the oyster and gently lift the oyster all around to expose any grit or shell pieces. Using your knife tip, flick any debris out onto the towel. (Picture D.)

7. Holding the shell firmly and starting on the inside rim of the shell, use the edge of your blade to detach the adductor muscle from the bottom shell. (Picture E.)

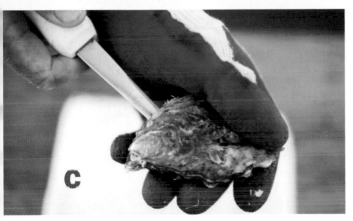

A Find the sweet spot.

B Wiggle the knife to pop the hinge.

C Rotate the oyster, sliding the knife into the oyster and back along the top shell to detach the top adductor muscle.

D Clean away any bits of shell or debris with the tip of the knife.

E Slide the knife under the oyster to free it from the bottom adductor muscle.

OYSTER KNIVES AND GLOVES: The Good, the Bad, and the Worthless

Ask any professional oyster shucker to discuss his knife, and you'll hear strains of opinionated devotion as he sings the praises of his tool. Like the soldier and his rifle, the oyster shucker and his knife are nothing without each other. One of Hog Island's best shuckers, Rich Golden, has shucked thousands of oysters in a single day. I've even witnessed Rich shucking behind his back, just to show off. You don't want to get in the way when Rich is shucking, and you should never ask to borrow his knife, a Dexter-Russell S-122. Mike Watchorn, cofounder of Hog Island Oyster Company, has been shucking for twenty-seven years and readily admits that he's not nearly as fast as Rich, but he's still partial to his knife, a Dexter-Russell S-120, which he grinds to a frightening point. At the Hog Island Oyster Bar in San Francisco, the shuckers use Dexter-Russell knives too, and they are so sharp and pointed that they resemble stilettos. Don't try this kind of knife modification at home until you've safely shucked a few bushels of oysters.

My own favorite oyster knife is a Dexter-Russell S-120 that I've modified by sharpening the blade edge and point to easily cut through the adductor muscle and get into the hinge. I also use a Russell Harrington $2^3/_4$-inch blade with a slightly curved tip. The second knife is for shucking Hog Island's waning supply of French Hogs (the European flat oysters they grow). But a stock knife—the type I'm going to recommend—and the right technique will get you through dozens of oysters with ease.

In the United States, there is a long history associated with oyster knives and blade pattern names that reflect the many traditions of oystering: the Boston Stabber and the Chesapeake Stabber had rounded wooden handles that fit securely into the palm of the hand, and long, narrow, tempered blades for shucking comfortably and efficiently. The Galveston knife was adapted for the big Gulf oysters, with a wooden handle that could be gripped with the whole hand and a long, substantial blade for breaking into the hard shells of larger oysters. The West Coast knives of yore were designed for the small, flat Olympia oyster, and with those gems in very short supply, these little knives with their sissy guards have been rendered useless.

Gloves protect your hand from the sharp edges of oyster shells. No glove will turn a forcefully wielded oyster knife. To avoid injury, learn good shucking technique, be patient, and practice safe shucking—never, ever, shuck without protection.

The Good

A good oyster knife has a well-tempered blade that's $2^3/_4$ to 4 inches long and a rugged handle that fits well in your hand. In my opinion, the best oyster knives are made by the Dexter-Russell company, located in Southbridge, Massachusetts, which has been manufacturing knives since 1818.

For shucking down, you need only one glove, and it isn't made of chain mail or silicone; it's a simple combination of knit and rubberized material and can be found at your local hardware or gardening store. The brand I like to use is called Boss, and for under $10, according to their sales material, you'll get "a knit body with [a] blue latex shell [that] makes for an unusually snug fit for a latex glove." Knit-latex gloves give you a good grip, and they are durable and low-maintenance. You can wash your glove at the kitchen sink and let it dry over your oyster knife handle. You'll get a pair, but if you're right-handed, you'll only need the left glove, and vice versa if you're left-handed.

For shucking in-hand, pair the rubberized Boss glove with a leather-palmed glove (an old cycling glove works best). Take care; even the double protection with the leather palm won't prevent an oyster knife from slicing into your hand.

The Bad

I have been horrified when I've come across sections on oyster-shucking in some cookbooks that say you can shuck an oyster with a stout paring knife or a screwdriver if you don't have an oyster knife. Please don't do this. Most cooking knife blades are not strong enough to stand up against the shell, and using a screwdriver is a prelude to a trip to the emergency room.

The Worthless

When you're shopping for an oyster knife, steer clear of anything that's shorter than $2^1/_2$ inches, and don't buy a knife with one of those silly metal guards. Stubby knives can't get you in all the way, and the guard is completely unnecessary if you learn to handle your oyster properly. If you combine a short blade with a guard, you have a truly worthless oyster knife.

The slinky chain mail gloves that come from France fail to protect your hand from the sharp tip of the oyster knife and cost close to $150 for one glove. I saw a professional shucker skewer his hand while wearing one—not a pretty sight. Other oyster-shucking tools to avoid: fancy and overpriced silicone oyster "gloves" that look like they belong in a puppet show for toddlers, and V-shaped wood oyster implements that ostensibly restrain your oyster so you can attack it with a knife. Trust me, an oyster is a gentle creature that tends to lie very still when placed on a counter. You'll have much more control if you just hold it on your shucking surface with a kitchen towel.

WHAT TO DRINK WITH RAW OYSTERS

Wine

Without exception, all raw oysters share primary flavor characteristics: briny, crisp, fresh, and salty. The secondary flavors depend on the oyster species, the environment, and the season, which factors can add buttery, smoky, melon, cucumber, and metallic (coppery) nuances. But the primary flavors will predominate, and that's what you're dealing with when matching raw oysters and wine. The goal is to achieve a synergistic harmony of flavors between the wine you choose and your oysters, and since wines are neither briny nor salty, you'll want to stay with varietals that are crisp and fresh. If a wine is crisp, it will have the appropriate amount of acidity—a wine's version of a squeeze of lemon on food—to stand up to the briny, salty flavor of the oyster. If I asked you the color of a crisp wine, you will undoubtedly say white. But not just any old white wine will do. Be choosy, and you'll find some wonderful companions for your oysters. The wines below, beginning with the most popular and ending with a couple of surprises, will get you through dozens of oysters.

Sauvignon Blanc

By far the most popular wine to serve with oysters is Sauvignon Blanc. The natural high acidity of the grape delivers a tangy, zesty, and crisp flavor that cuts through the brine and pairs beautifully with all oysters. The French appellations Sancerre and Pouilly-Fumé represent the best of the Sauvignon Blanc grape: pure, straightforward, and sassy.

Pinot Gris

A summertime favorite, Pinot Gris is a light, refreshing wine that pairs well with milder—that is, not overly salty—oysters. The style of this varietal can vary from light and crisp to floral. For the best pairing with oysters, try to stay with the light and crisp styles. Your best bet is to choose a domestic, not European, producer. California Pinot Gris wines (some of which are called Pinot Grigio) are almost certain to deliver the fresh, crisp taste you're looking for.

Chablis

Don't confuse this wonderfully refreshing and sophisticated French wine with the California jug wines of the last century. Made from Chardonnay grapes in the northernmost region of Burgundy, this is one of the best wines to pair with oysters. An interesting fact for oyster lovers is that the best Chablis vineyards are full of fossilized oyster shells. As master sommelier Andrea Immer says in her book *Great Wine Made Simple*, "With bivalves, who needs a squeeze of lemon when you have Chablis?"

Albariño

From the largest seafood-producing area in Europe, the region of Galicia in the northwesternmost corner of Spain, comes one of the best wines I have ever had with oysters: Albariño. This dry white wine is one of Spain's most distinctive. Aromatic with prominent citrus notes and delightfully fresh flavors, Albariños are, in my opinion, the best wines to enjoy with the slightly sweet and smoky Pacific oyster.

Champagne and Sparkling Wine

Champagne, oysters, and caviar are clichéd indulgences of the idle rich. Be that as it may, I encourage you to heap luxury upon luxury and place a spoonful of caviar on an oyster and wash it down with Champagne. Then do it again. I am so fond of Champagne that if I could get away with it, I'd be sipping it all day long, and it is a nearly perfect match with my other obsession: oysters.

To be called Champagne, a wine must come from the Champagne region of France, about ninety miles northeast of Paris. The best type of Champagne to enjoy with oysters is a *blanc de blancs* ("white from whites"), which means that it is made entirely of Chardonnay grapes. The result is a light, complex, and elegant wine that meets the briny oyster face-to-face, tickling the palate with bubbles that cut through the salt and accentuate the subtler flavors. The experience is like the grand finale of a great fireworks show—in your mouth. The best *blanc de blancs* Champagnes are made by Taittinger, Salon, and Krug.

In the United States, wines made with the Champagne method are supposed to be called sparkling wines, and no one but an oenophile or a French Champagne maker is going to care if you slip and call your Domaine Chandon Mt. Veeder *blanc de blancs* sparkler "champagne." There are many good domestic sparkling wines to enjoy with oysters: Iron Horse, Gloria Ferrer, Roederer Estate, Schramsberg, and the aforementioned Domaine Chandon. If you're not drinking a *blanc de blancs*, stick with a brut, which is not too dry and not too sweet.

Beer

A few years ago I attended a brewmaster's dinner, where each of the seven courses, including dessert, was paired with a different beer. I left the dinner uncomfortably full but with a whole new perspective on pairing beer with oysters. Beer and oysters is a pairing seventeen hundred years older than that of Champagne and oysters. In parts of Ireland and now in the United States, oyster and beer festivals have become a tradition.

The classic pairing is a dry Irish-style stout, and this has become such a popular combination that there's actually a stout with oysters brewed right in it. The custom of drinking stout with oysters comes from the pubs around the docks of London, where yesteryear's blue-collar workers could slam down a couple dozen oysters and a few pints without breaking the bank. This is a pairing in contrasts, and while not the most sophisticated marriage, it is traditional.

Beer is made primarily from water, barley malt, hops, and yeast. The cereal part of the beer, together with the yeast, gives beer its flavor, color, and body. Hops give beer its pleasant bitterness, which to beer is what acidity is to wine: that essential component that rounds out saltiness and enhances subtle flavors. Lagers tend to have a crisper flavor profile than ales, and a lightly hopped lager such as Sam Adams's Light is great with oysters. If you're not sure, stay with beers that say lager, and shy away from any beer that is fuller bodied or slightly sweet.

OYSTERS AND LOVE

If you skipped over the rest of this book and turned directly to this section, then congratulations—you're a true oyster-lover, but you probably already knew that. There's a tingle you get when you eat a plate of raw oysters, a gleam in the eye, a restlessness, a . . . well, you know. And so did the Romans, who served hundreds of raw oysters before and, it is said, during their orgies. Napoleon fortified himself with oysters before going into battle, illuminating the connection between the battlefield and the bedroom—after all, it takes testosterone to perform in either venue. That paragon of love, Giacomo Casanova, not only downed dozens of oysters for breakfast, he and his lovers employed them in other creative ways, as he recorded in his memoirs:

> Then came the oyster-game, and I scolded Armelline for having swallowed the liquid as I was taking the oyster from her lips. I agreed that it was very hard to avoid doing so, but I offered to shew them how it could be done by placing the tongue in the way. This gave me an opportunity of teaching them the game of tongues, which I shall not explain because it is well known to all true lovers. . . . It so chanced that a fine oyster slipped from its shell as I was placing it between Emilie's lips. It fell on to her breast, and she would have recovered it with her fingers; but I claimed the right of regaining it myself, and she had to unlace her bodice to let me do so. . . . "I want my oyster," said I. "Take it, then." There was no need to tell me twice. I unlaced her corset in such a way as to make it fall still lower, bewailing the necessity of having to search for it with my hands. What a martyrdom for an amorous man to have to conceal his bliss at such a moment!

Oysters were often served in nineteenth-century brothels, either for their libido-enhancing qualities, or perhaps because at that time they were a mainstay of the working man's diet. Whatever the case, from Roman times to the present, oysters have been closely aligned with lust and licentious behavior. In my oyster classes I try to address the subject before any of my students feel compelled to bring it up. I generally pose a question to the class such as, "How many of you have heard that oysters are an aphrodisiac?" Everyone raises his or her hand. Then I ask, "How many of you actually believe that oysters are an aphrodisiac?" The raised hands are reduced by half, because in our culture who wants to publicly reveal secrets about their libido? If the group seems up for it, I'll call on one of those raised hands and ask that brave person to share his or her experience. Usually there's a round

Man becomes amorous through the senses, which, touch excepted, all reside in the head.

GIACOMO CASANOVA

of nervous laughter, some blushing, and an expurgated story. After we've broken the ice, I tell the class that whether or not the Food and Drug Administration wants to admit it or not, oysters *do* have aphrodisiac qualities.

An aphrodisiac is a food, drink, drug, or scent that is reputed to arouse or increase sexual desire or libido. The word derives from the name of Aphrodite, the Greek goddess of love and beauty, and the list of supposed sex-enhancing and sexually stimulating foods includes asparagus, anchovies, chilies, chocolate, curries, licorice, scallops, vanilla, and oysters, to name just a few.

Hard science practitioners (including the FDA) usually dismiss aphrodisiacs as folk remedies. However, oysters do have a very high concentration of zinc, which is a chemical precursor to testosterone, a sex hormone produced by both women and men. Recently, a study by a team of American and Italian researchers presented some very interesting information on bivalves, includ-

ing oysters, to the American Chemical Society at a conference in San Diego. They found two unusual amino acids in the shellfish: D-aspartic acid (D-Asp) and N-methyl-D-aspartate (NMDA). After isolating the amino acids, the researchers injected them into laboratory rats and found that the acids triggered testosterone production in male rats and progesterone production in female rats.

If centuries of tradition and suggestive new science can't persuade you of oysters' power to stimulate the senses, you may just have to see for yourself. Inside the fortress of the oyster shell is a beautiful, shimmering creature that is primarily a sex organ. So open an oyster and free it from its pearly bed with your fingers or the tip of your oyster knife. Turn it one quarter turn until it's lying on its side. Ponder its beauty and its similarities to a part of the human anatomy, then slurp it down lustily. I guarantee you'll feel a tingle somewhere.

CHAPTER 4

RAW OYSTERS

When you order a half-dozen oysters on the half shell, at most restaurants your order will come with just a condiment cup of vinegary mignonette or cocktail sauce and a wedge of lemon. More inspired restaurants and chefs play with the mutability of the oyster, creating savvy, sexy toppings for raw oysters. I've included some of the best here: a lemony granita embellished with caviar, a snappy habanero mignonette, an Asian medley of spices and garlic, and the ever-popular Hogwash. You'll also find other recipes with ingredients and flavors that you may not have thought of before—try them and enjoy the surprise. And don't be afraid to experiment on your own.

Plan on serving 4 to 6 raw oysters per person for an appetizer or first course. In this chapter, I have usually written the recipes to yield enough topping for 2 or 3 dozen oysters—usually Pacific extra-smalls (2 to 3 inches long) or Eastern smalls (3 to 4 inches long). If you are serving more or fewer, the ratio of oysters to topping is easy to adjust—a teaspoon or less of topping per oyster is about right.

Hogwash and Sweetwaters 84

Hog Island Cocktail Sauce with Oysters on the Half Shell 85

Oysters and Classic Mignonette Sauce 86

Oysters with Raspberry Mignonette 88

Oysters with Cucumber, Lime, and Sake 90

Pacific Oysters with Sesame Vinaigrette 92

Champagne Mignonette and Oysters 93

Oysters with Ginger-Lime Vinaigrette 94

Oysters Topped with Sriracha Sauce, Lime, and Lemongrass 95

Pacific Oysters with Lemon Ice and Caviar 97

Oysters with Citrus Relish 99

Oysters on the Half Shell with Pickled Fennel Topping 100

Raw Oysters and Balsamic Mignonette 101

Oysters with Lemon Crème Fraîche and Caviar 102

Rémoulade Sauce with Oysters 103

Oyster Shooters with Tequila and Lime 104

Oyster Shots with Ponzu Sauce 106

HOGWASH AND SWEETWATERS

HOGWASH

¼ cup seasoned rice vinegar

¼ cup unseasoned rice vinegar

1 large shallot, minced

1 large jalapeño chili, seeded and minced

Leaves from ½ bunch cilantro, finely chopped

Juice of 1 lime

3 dozen extra-small (2 to 3 inches long) Pacific or small (3 to 4 inches long) Eastern oysters on the half shell, on a bed of crushed ice

A savory variation on the classic mignonette sauce—a vinegar and shallot topping for oysters—this sauce was developed by Mark Miller of Santa Fe's Coyote Cafe. Michael Watchorn, cofounder of Hog Island Oyster Company, riffed on Mark's original, adding cilantro and jalapeño, and it has since become Hog Island's signature topping. The mixture of unseasoned and seasoned rice vinegar gives it the perfect balance of acidity and sweetness. Seasoned rice vinegar has sugar and salt added in just the right proportions. Both vinegars are great condiments to have on hand.

Note: The Hogwash should be served the day it is made.

In a medium bowl, combine all the ingredients except for the oysters. Just before serving, stir the mixture to make sure you pick up all the goodies in the bowl. Top each oyster with a teaspoonful of the sauce. Serve immediately.

| Makes 36 |

HOG ISLAND COCKTAIL SAUCE WITH OYSTERS ON THE HALF SHELL

HOG ISLAND COCKTAIL SAUCE

1 cup ketchup, preferably Heinz

1 tablespoon grated fresh horseradish

1 tablespoon fresh lemon juice

1 tablespoon seasoned rice vinegar

1 tablespoon Worcestershire sauce

1 teaspoon Tabasco sauce

3 dozen extra-small (2 to 3 inches long) Pacific or small (3 to 4 inches long) Eastern oysters on the half shell, on a bed of crushed ice

I admit I'm not a big fan of ordinary cocktail sauce on oysters, but a little of this fresh, homemade sauce on a chilled Hog Island Sweetwater (a Pacific oyster variety) is really good. Try not to smother your oyster with the sauce—a little goes a long way. Small Eastern oysters can also be used in this recipe.

In a small bowl, whisk together all the cocktail sauce ingredients. Spoon $1/2$ teaspoon of sauce on each oyster. Serve immediately.

| Makes 36 |

OYSTERS AND CLASSIC MIGNONETTE SAUCE

CLASSIC MIGNONETTE SAUCE

¾ cup red wine vinegar

¼ cup apple cider vinegar

2 teaspoons fresh lemon juice

2 dozen extra-small (2 to 3 inches long) Pacific or small (3 to 4 inches long) Eastern oysters on the half shell, on a bed of crushed ice

¼ cup minced shallots

1 tablespoon cracked pepper

After a simple squeeze of lemon, a mignonette sauce is the classic topping for raw oysters. This one uses two vinegars: red wine and apple cider. The apple cider vinegar mellows the bracing edge of the red wine vinegar, and the lemon juice lends just the right amount of tartness. Garnishing the oysters with shallots instead of mixing them into the liquid guarantees equal portions.

In a small bowl, combine all the sauce ingredients. Spoon 1 teaspoon of the mixture onto each oyster, and garnish each with a sprinkle of shallots and a pinch of cracked pepper. Serve immediately.

| Makes 24 |

OYSTERS WITH RASPBERRY MIGNONETTE

RASPBERRY MIGNONETTE

¾ cup commercial or homemade raspberry vinegar (recipe follows)

1 teaspoon sugar

1 tablespoon fresh lemon juice

2 dozen extra-small (2 to 3 inches long) Pacific or small (3 to 4 inches long) Eastern oysters on the half shell, on a bed of crushed ice

¼ cup minced fresh chives

Raspberry vinegar is a wonderful condiment to have on hand, and its fruity character brings out the sweetness in Pacific oysters. The deep pink color of this mignonette, together with the chive garnish, is a sexy presentation on silvery oysters. Try this on Valentine's Day and test the aphrodisiac theory. Raspberry vinegar is available in better grocery stores, but if you plan ahead, you can make your own with the recipe opposite.

In a small bowl, combine all the mignonette ingredients. Spoon 1 teaspoon of the mixture onto each oyster and garnish each with a sprinkle of chives. Serve immediately.

| Makes 24 |

RASPBERRY VINEGAR

Fill a sterilized 1-quart canning jar with fresh raspberries to within 2 inches of the rim. (You will need 2 pint baskets of raspberries.) Add distilled white vinegar to cover the berries. Add 3 strips lemon zest, 2 thyme sprigs, and 8 peppercorns. Seal and set on a kitchen counter out of direct sunlight until the liquid turns raspberry red, about 1 week. Strain into a 1-quart bottle. Store in a cool, dry place. Will keep for 12 months.

OYSTERS WITH CUCUMBER, LIME, AND SAKE

2 dozen extra-small (2 to 3 inches long) Pacific or small (3 to 4 inches long) Eastern oysters on the half shell, on a bed of crushed ice

1 cucumber, peeled, seeded, and shredded

6 limes, quartered

1¾ cups chilled dry sake

Rodney's Oyster House in Toronto, Canada, is famous for the variety of fresh oysters they serve. Rodney himself holds one of the first oyster-shucking titles in the region. This refreshing oyster appetizer features an unusual combination of flavors in perfect balance.

Top each oyster with a pinch of shredded cucumber. Squeeze a lime quarter over each oyster. Carefully pour sake over each oyster, just to the rim of the shell. Serve immediately.

| Makes 24 |

PACIFIC OYSTERS WITH SESAME VINAIGRETTE

SESAME VINAIGRETTE

2 tablespoons packed
light brown sugar

1/2 teaspoon freshly
ground pepper

1/4 cup fresh lime juice

1/4 cup seasoned rice vinegar

3 tablespoons mirin (rice wine)

3 tablespoons tamari
soy sauce

1/4 cup canola oil

2 teaspoons toasted
sesame oil

2 dozen extra-small
(2 to 3 inches long) Pacific
(preferable) or small
(3 to 4 inches long) Eastern
oysters on the half shell,
on a bed of crushed ice

3 tablespoons sesame seeds,
toasted

My brother-in-law, Ron Parisi, works for a major airline and has been flying the Los Angeles/Honolulu route for a number of years. On his layovers in Honolulu, he surfs and eats—in that order. An innovative cook and confessed oyster junkie, he created this vinaigrette after a Japanese food binge on the north shore of Oahu. There's something about the salty-sweet combinations in Asian cooking that makes this vinaigrette a perfect topping for briny oysters. The toasted sesame oil in this sauce overpowers the milder Eastern oysters, so use Pacifics if you can.

In a medium bowl, whisk together the sugar, pepper, lime juice, rice vinegar, mirin, and tamari until the sugar is dissolved. In a measuring cup, stir the oils together. Gradually whisk the oil mixture into the vinegar mixture. Spoon 1 teaspoon onto each oyster and garnish with the toasted sesame seeds. Serve immediately.

| **Makes 24** |

CHAMPAGNE MIGNONETTE AND OYSTERS

¾ cup brut Champagne or sparkling white wine

3 tablespoons sugar

2 dozen extra-small (2 to 3 inches long) Pacific or small (3 to 4 inches long) Eastern oysters on the half shell, on a bed of crushed ice

¼ cup minced shallots

2 tablespoons cracked pepper

The food at the Olema Inn Restaurant is so good that it's hard for me not to go there at least once a week. When I go, I always have Chef Ed Vigil's Hog Island oysters with Champagne mignonette. When I called for the recipe, Ed was on his honeymoon in the Caribbean. I didn't want to bother him, so here's a close approximation of his recipe. If you're opening a bottle of bubbly, you might as well enjoy the rest of it with these oysters.

In a small bowl, combine the wine and sugar, stirring gently to dissolve the sugar. Spoon 1 teaspoon of the sauce onto each oyster and garnish each with a sprinkle of shallots and a pinch of cracked pepper. Serve immediately.

| Makes 24 |

OYSTERS WITH GINGER-LIME VINAIGRETTE

GINGER-LIME VINAIGRETTE

¼ cup canola oil

6 tablespoons fresh lime juice

6 tablespoons unseasoned rice vinegar

2 teaspoons tamari soy sauce

2 teaspoons Thai chili sauce

1 small clove garlic, minced

1 tablespoon grated fresh ginger

2 dozen extra-small (2 to 3 inches long) Pacific or small (3 to 4 inches long) Eastern oysters on the half shell, on a bed of crushed ice

24 fresh cilantro leaves

Oyster flavors perk up when they meet ginger and citrus, and adding Thai chili sauce kicks in another flavor dimension. Thai chili sauce isn't flame-throwing hot; it's mildly spicy and sweet, with a little citrus note. I like the Thai Kitchen brand, which is available in most grocery specialty aisles. The fresh cilantro adds color, and its pungency rounds out the vinaigrette.

In a blender or food processor, combine all the vinaigrette ingredients. Puree for 30 seconds, or until smooth. Spoon 1 teaspoon of the vinaigrette over each oyster and garnish with a cilantro leaf. Serve immediately.

| Makes 24 |

OYSTERS TOPPED WITH SRIRACHA SAUCE, LIME, AND LEMONGRASS

½ cup sriracha sauce

¼ cup fresh lime juice

1 tablespoon sugar

2 dozen extra-small (2 to 3 inches long) Pacific or small (3 to 4 inches long) Eastern oysters on the half shell, on a bed of crushed ice

3 tablespoons minced fresh lemongrass

I discovered sriracha sauce on the table of a breakfast dive in North San Juan, California, a tiny town in the north Sierra foothills. I put it on my scrambled eggs and home fries. Why not oysters? I thought. Sriracha is a spicy-sweet chili sauce from Southeast Asia; if you can't pronounce it, just call it rooster sauce (for the rooster on the label of a widely available brand).

Lemongrass is also something I always have on hand. It's an aromatic, grasslike herb, also originally from Southeast Asia, and it contains the same substance that makes lemons taste like lemons. You can find it in Asian grocery stores and in many major supermarkets.

In a small bowl, combine the sriracha sauce, lime juice, and sugar. Stir well to blend. Spoon 1 teaspoon sauce on each oyster. Garnish with a sprinkle of lemongrass. Serve immediately.

| Makes 24 |

95

OYSTERS WITH LEMON ICE AND CAVIAR

LEMON ICE

¼ teaspoon grated Meyer lemon zest

1 cup fresh Meyer lemon juice

¼ cup sparkling water

1½ dozen extra-small (2 to 3 inches long) Pacific or small (3 to 4 inches long) Eastern oysters on the half shell, on a bed of crushed ice

2 ounces caviar, preferably from California

Chervil sprigs for garnish

The combination of the subtle Meyer lemon ice and the intense pop of caviar make this a multilayered sense experience. Meyer lemons have a sweeter and less acidic juice than regular lemons. It's fine to substitute regular lemons, but the flavor of the oyster may be overpowered by the acid. This recipe comes from Chad Callahan, former executive chef of San Francisco's famed Masa's restaurant.

In a 9-by-13-inch baking dish, combine all the lemon ice ingredients. Freeze for 4 hours.

Remove the frozen mixture from the freezer and, using the tines of a fork, scrape it into a bowl until it has the texture of a snow cone. Spoon 1 teaspoon of the lemon ice on top of each oyster. Top with ¼ teaspoon caviar and a sprig of chervil. Serve immediately.

| **Makes 18** |

VARIATIONS:

• Substitute ¼ cup good vodka for ¼ cup of the lemon juice.

• Substitute ¼ cup Pernod for the lemon zest and juice. Increase the sparkling water to ½ cup.

OYSTERS WITH CITRUS RELISH

1 lemon, scrubbed

1 small orange, scrubbed

1 small grapefruit, scrubbed

1 teaspoon sugar

1 shallot, minced

1 teaspoon light olive oil

Salt and freshly ground pepper to taste

2 dozen extra-small (2 to 3 inches long) Pacific oysters or small (3 to 4 inches long) Eastern oysters on the half shell, on a bed of crushed ice

Out on the edge of the world in Olema, California, near Tomales Bay, is a remarkable restaurant called the Olema Inn. Chef Ed Vigil's menu reflects the abundance of foods grown locally, and his recipes are innovative and inspiring. Oysters with citrus relish is one of my favorites. Make sure you grate the zest finely—I use my indispensable Microplane, which I think every cook should have in the kitchen.

Using a Microplane or the finest rasps of a box grater, grate the zest of the lemon, orange, and grapefruit onto a plate and set aside. Juice the lemon, orange, and one half of the grapefruit and strain the juice through a fine-meshed sieve into a small bowl. You should have about $^1/_3$ cup juice. Add the sugar and stir to dissolve. Pour into a small saucepan and cook over medium-low heat until reduced by half, about 15 minutes.

In a medium bowl, combine the citrus zest, reduced juice, shallot, oil, salt, and pepper. Refrigerate for 15 minutes.

Stir the sauce to distribute any zest or shallot that has settled. Spoon 1 teaspoon sauce on top of each oyster and serve immediately.

| **Makes 24** |

OYSTERS ON THE HALF SHELL WITH PICKLED FENNEL TOPPING

PICKLED FENNEL STEMS

9 fennel stems (from 2 to 3 fennel bulbs)

1 teaspoon red pepper flakes

1 tablespoon fennel seeds

1 teaspoon juniper berries

1 teaspoon coriander seeds

1 teaspoon kosher salt

2 cups unseasoned rice vinegar

1½ dozen extra-small (2 to 3 inches long) Pacific or small (3 to 4 inches long) Eastern oysters on the half shell, on a bed of crushed ice

Fennel imparts a wonderfully subtle anise flavor to shellfish and goes especially well with oysters. In this recipe from Paul Arenstam, chef of Belon, in San Francisco, the mildly acidic rice vinegar, together with the crunch of the fennel stems, gives raw oysters an intriguing balance of flavor and texture. Save the fennel bulbs for a salad or braising—they will keep for up to 2 weeks in the vegetable drawer of your refrigerator.

Note: You will need to start the pickled fennel stems 1 day ahead of serving.

Cut the fennel stems into $1/2$-inch matchsticks and put them in a medium bowl. Set aside.

In a small saucepan, combine all the remaining ingredients (except the oysters) and cook over medium-high heat until the liquid boils, about 3 minutes. Reduce the heat to low and simmer for an additional 10 minutes to combine the flavors. Pour the hot liquid over the fennel stems. Cover and refrigerate for 24 hours.

To serve, top each oyster with 1 teaspoon of the pickled fennel stems and a drop of the flavored vinegar.

| Makes 18 |

RAW OYSTERS AND BALSAMIC MIGNONETTE

BALSAMIC MIGNONETTE

¼ cup good-quality balsamic vinegar

¼ cup soy sauce

¼ cup fresh lemon juice

1 teaspoon sugar

2 dozen extra-small (2 to 3 inches long) Pacific or small (3 to 4 inches long) Eastern oysters on the half shell, on a bed of crushed ice

¼ cup minced red bell pepper

¼ cup finely chopped green onion, green parts included

In this twist on a traditional mignonette, the balsamic vinegar brings out the sweetness in oysters. The lemon juice adds crispness, and the soy sauce rounds out the complex flavors. Use a good-quality regular balsamic vinegar—not the very expensive aged kind. The garnish of minced red pepper and green onion makes a bright contrast with the silvery oysters.

In a medium bowl, mix together all the ingredients for the mignonette. Spoon 1 teaspoon of the mignonette over each oyster. Garnish with the bell pepper and green onion. Serve immediately.

| Makes 24 |

OYSTERS WITH LEMON CRÈME FRAÎCHE AND CAVIAR

½ cup crème fraîche

1 tablespoon grated lemon zest

2 dozen extra-small (2 to 3 inches long) Pacific or small (3 to 4 inches long) Eastern oysters on the half shell, on a bed of crushed ice

2 ounces caviar, preferably from California

24 julienne strips lemon zest (see Note)

Crème fraîche has just the right amount of tanginess to go perfectly with oysters. The lemon zest brings out the best flavors in the oyster, and the pop of the caviar adds another touch of saltiness.

In a small bowl, combine the crème fraîche and grated lemon zest. Top each oyster with 1 teaspoon of the crème fraîche mixture, then a small dollop of caviar. Garnish with strips of lemon zest. Serve immediately.

| Makes 24 |

Note: To make the julienne garnish, strip the zest from a lemon with a vegetable peeler, then cut the strips of zest into matchsticks with a sharp chef's knife. If you're not going to use the garnish right away, drop the pieces into ice water to keep them crisp.

RÉMOULADE SAUCE WITH OYSTERS

RÉMOULADE SAUCE

1 hard-cooked egg yolk

1 tablespoon Dijon mustard

1 cup Best Foods or Hellmann's mayonnaise

1 tablespoon Worcestershire sauce

1 tablespoon sweet paprika

Dash of Tabasco sauce

2 tablespoons red wine vinegar

¼ cup minced fresh flat-leaf parsley

¼ teaspoon freshly ground pepper

2 dozen extra-small (2 to 3 inches long) Pacific or small (3 to 4 inches long) Eastern oysters on the half shell, on a bed of crushed ice

This version of the classic sauce for cold seafood is a rich, delicious topping for raw oysters. Dijon mustard and Worcestershire sauce add a little bite, and the anchovies in the original sauce are omitted, as the oysters contribute just the right amount of salt.

Push the egg yolk through a fine meshed sieve into a medium bowl. Add all the remaining sauce ingredients and stir to blend. Cover and refrigerate for 1 hour. Spoon ½ to 1 teaspoon on each oyster. Serve immediately.

| **Makes 24** |

OYSTER SHOOTERS WITH TEQUILA AND LIME

Extra-small (2 to 3 inches long) Pacific or small (3 to 4 inches long) Eastern oysters on the half shell, on a bed of crushed ice

Tabasco sauce

Tequila

Limes

Fresh horseradish root, grated

No one really knows who invented oyster shooters, but this inspired oyster appetizer surely followed in the footsteps of the infamous tequila shooter, as the technique is the same. Thankfully, unless you're very liberal with the tequila you probably won't wake up with a wicked hangover from a dozen of these. If you're serving shooters as an appetizer, count 4 to 6 per person. If you're just having oysters, well, don't stop until you're satisfied.

For each shooter, put an oyster into a shot glass and add one of the following: a few shakes of Tabasco sauce, a splash of tequila, a squeeze of a quartered lime, or $^1/_4$ to $^1/_2$ teaspoon freshly grated horseradish. Shoot!

OYSTER SHOTS WITH PONZU SAUCE

PONZU SAUCE

1 cup soy sauce

¾ cup fresh lemon juice

¼ cup rice vinegar

½ cup dried bonito flakes

1 teaspoon grated lemon zest

2 dozen extra-small (2 to 3 inches long) Pacific or small (3 to 4 inches long) Eastern oysters on the half shell, on a bed of crushed ice

Hiro Sone and his wife, Lissa Doumani, own Terra in Napa Valley and Ame in San Francisco and are longtime friends of Hog Island. Pairing ponzu, a classic Japanese sauce, with freshly shucked oysters was Hiro's idea, and the combination of salt, citrus, and subtle smokiness is a brilliant match.

Bonito flakes are not a fishy breakfast cereal—the flakes are made from high-quality bonito, which is steamed, aged, air-dried, and then cut into delicate shavings. It's a wonderful ingredient to have on hand and adds a delicious, rich, smoky flavor to dishes. For the best sauce, make it the day before so the flavors marry.

In a small ceramic or glass bowl, combine all the sauce ingredients. Cover and refrigerate overnight.

Strain the sauce, then shuck and drain the oysters. To serve, put each oyster in a shot glass and spoon 1 teaspoon of the sauce over the oyster. Nestle the shot glasses into a bed of crushed ice on a platter.

| Makes 24 |

CHAPTER 5

HOT OYSTERS

When I first started eating oysters as a kid, my family ate them cooked. The most interesting thing my mom did was dip them in an egg wash, roll them in crushed saltines, and sauté them in butter—and those oysters disappeared as fast as she could cook them. You'll find that recipe here, but also a delicious collection of old and new ways to serve oysters hot. I chased down the authentic oysters Rockefeller recipe for you and kicked up a classic oyster stew but didn't stop there. Some celebrity chefs have a penchant for oysters and were willing to share their favorite recipes with us.

In this chapter I have suggested types and sizes of oysters that will work best in proportion to the other ingredients in each recipe. Some recipes call for Pacific oysters specifically; this is because their deeper-cupped bottom shells work better when individual oysters are served in the shell with hot toppings. For stews and soups, either Pacifics or Easterns can be used.

Crispy Oysters with Mango Sauce and Red Horseradish | 113
Deviled Fried Oysters with Spinach and Pancetta | 116
Chez Panisse Oyster Stew with Thyme and Fennel | 118
Steamed Oysters with Spicy Asian Sauce | 120
Poached Oysters with Crème Fraîche and Caviar | 121
Oysters Pablo | 122
Fried Oysters with Cilantro Aioli | 124
Oyster Soup, Thai Style | 125
Grilled Farm-Style Oysters | 126
Barbecued Oysters | 128
Oyster Stew with Chipotle Butter | 130
New England–Style Oyster and Clam Chowder | 133
Oyster and Shrimp Gumbo | 134
Hangtown Fry | 136
The Real Oysters Rockefeller | 139
Farmers' Market Oyster Po' Boy | 141

continued

Oysters with Chorizo and White Beans | 144
Buttery Pan-Fried Oysters | 146
Serrano Ham–Wrapped Oysters with Chipotle Mayonnaise | 147
Angels on Horseback | 148
Chanterelle and Parmesan Oysters | 151
Oysters Casino | 152
Peacemaker Loaf | 153

There are three kinds of oyster-eaters: those loose-minded sports who will eat anything, hot, cold, thin, thick, dead, or alive, as long as it is oyster; those who will eat them raw and only raw; those who with equal severity eat them cooked and no other way.

M. F. K. FISHER

CRISPY OYSTERS WITH MANGO SAUCE AND RED HORSERADISH

MANGO SAUCE

1 ripe mango, peeled, pitted, and coarsely chopped

3 tablespoons fresh lime juice

3 tablespoons coarsely chopped red onion

2 cloves garlic, coarsely chopped

1 teaspoon Tabasco sauce

¼ cup canola oil

Salt and freshly ground pepper taste

Hot, hot, and sweet is the best description for chef Bobby Flay's Southwestern oyster appetizer. The mango sauce balances the snappy chili horseradish that tops each delectable cornmeal-crusted oyster. It's more than just a combination of wonderful spices: The colors in each shell look like a New Mexico sunset.

If you can't find fresh horseradish, prepared horseradish is fine, as long as you drain off some of the liquid. The mango sauce is so good that I've actually seen people lick the bottom of the shell to get the last drop. Serve the leftover sauce in a bowl alongside the appetizers so an extra dollop can be spooned on top.

FOR THE MANGO SAUCE: In a food processor, combine all the sauce ingredients except the salt and pepper. Process until smooth, about 1 minute. Season with salt and pepper.

continued on page 115

113